Louison

The Life and Loves of Marie Louise O'Morphi

Desmond Clarke

Blackstaff Press

Published by Blackstaff Press, 255A Upper Newtownards Road, Belfast BT4 3JF.

ISBN 0 85640 146 3

Contents

List of Illustrations

Preface

Louise O'Morphi, or simply Louise Murphy, has been immortalised by Boucher in many of his best known paintings; she finds honourable or dishonourable mention in the bawdy and lecherous memoirs of Casanova who failed to seduce her; and her name crops up continuously in the diaries of those attached in one capacity or another to the Court of Louis XV whose mistress she was. Despite her role in history, in art and in harlotry little is known about her. With the exception of a delightful little book by Patrick de Heriz, *La Belle O'Morphi*, which was published privately in 1947, there is no other authentic record of her strange story, hence a valid excuse for this short work.

I am indebted to a number of people for helping me to winnow fact from fiction, particularly members of the staff of the Bibliothèque Nationale in Paris, Mr J. A. Roe who so carefully checked the entire text and made many important corrections, and I am grateful to Una McLaughlin who typed the final text for the printers.

Finally I wish to acknowledge my indebtedness to Messrs Longman Green for permission to quote from W. R. Trist's translation of *The Memoirs of Casanova* published in 1967, the proprietors of the *Burlington Magazine*, Jean Cailleux of the Galerie Cailleux Paris, the Trustees of the Wallace Collection London, the Musée des Beaux-Arts, Rheims, and Alte Pinakothek, Munich.

Desmond Clarke

The Shoemaker's Daughters

The ancient city of Rouen has had long associations with Ireland. From the earliest times bands of Irishmen, marauding sailors, gentle missioners, soldiers of fortune, refugees and skilled craftsmen, unable to find work at home, settled there. The first large wave of soldiers and refugees arrived in Rouen at the beginning of the seventeenth century following the Elizabethan conquest and settlement of parts of Ireland. Less than fifty years later another exodus occurred after the Cromwellian conquest of the country, and the wholesale confiscation of the lands and homes of Irish nobles. Towards the end of the century, after the final defeat of the Irish adherents of the Stuart cause, many thousand Irishmen, under the terms of the Treaty of Limerick, chose exile to poverty at home, and as the famed 'Wild Geese' became soldiers of fortune in the armies of France, Spain and other European countries.

Among the Irish exiles who settled in Rouen at this time was one Daniel Murphy, or O'Murphy, described as a former Jacobite soldier who served in the army of James II in Ireland, and then sailed to France after the defeat at Limerick. He has also been described as a member of a noble Irish family which emigrated to France and sought refuge there during the reign of James I, following the Crown policy of confiscation and settlement in the first decade of the seventeenth century. A third and possibly more correct surmise is that he was a shoemaker or saddler in the French army — just one of the many ordinary Irishmen who found refuge and a new life in France after the Treaty of Limerick in 1691.

Daniel Murphy may have been a soldier, but by the 1720s he was well settled in the city of Rouen and carried on the trade of a shoemaker, cobbler and saddler. At this time he was married to a compatriot named Margaret Hickey, who, in the light of subsequent events, might have been in her earlier years a camp-follower.

1

In the course of time the Irish cobbler of Rouen fathered five daughters. Few such men have had the honour, dubious or otherwise, of fathering five lovely daughters whose names are now enshrined in the more curious and lesser known annals of French history. Indeed, but for his daughters the names of Daniel Murphy and Margaret Hickey would be of as little consequence as the names of the vast majority of the citizens of Rouen from the time of the ancient Rothomagus to the present day.

Life was not easy for the family, so to alleviate their poverty, Margaret Murphy, between childbirths, was a dealer in ladies' toilet accessories, and a peddler of old clothes. She was considerably younger than her husband but a shrewd woman of the world with plenty of drive, and not averse to turning a dishonest penny when and where she could. She had ambitions too for her daughters, and looked far beyond the tight, provincial town which offered little to a self-seeking woman with five daughters, and even less to pretty young women with a poor and humble background.

The first of the Murphy, or as they preferred to call themselves O'Morphi, girls was born about 1726, and was christened Marguerite. From babyhood she showed promise of real beauty, and was a gay, good-humoured and light-hearted child; one born to love and be loved. A little more than a year later a second daughter was born; and she was christened with the good Irish name of Brigitte; she was a somewhat plain child and lacked the vivacity of her sister Marguerite. An outstanding feature, however, of the child, and apparent from an early age, were her shapely hands, and these hands almost compensated for the plainness of her features, which were impaired in later years by very noticeable pockmarks.

About 1729, Margaret Murphy gave birth to her third child, still another daughter who was christened Madeline. Like her elder sister, Madeline was a pretty baby and as she grew to girlhood she became more and more attractive. She was a consummate little mimic and a natural actress, which made her popular with her playmates, whom she could entertain for hours on end with mimicry, dancing and acting, talents to be fully exploited in later years.

Towards the end of the following year a fourth child — Victoire — was born into the Murphy household. This dainty brunette whose slight pockmarks failed to detract from her beauty, had vivacious sparkling eyes which attracted much attention in later years. Victoire would have been almost a perfect model of feminine charms but for the treacherous rolls of fat even in womanhood made her legs somewhat ugly. But in these days of long and voluminous dresses this blemish was not readily visible, though on imaginable occasions it might hinder her successful advancement in the

2

career which seemed mapped out for the girls at the outset.

Though Daniel Murphy was growing old and his sight dimming with the years, he had to work harder than ever to provide for his growing household, and times were by no means easy. It was a period of depression in France, a depression that characterised the last years of the reign of Louis XIV, and was even more serious during the final years of Fleury's ministry under the young king Louis XV, when his subjects in Paris greeted him with cries of *misère, du pain, du pain*, and forced open the doors of Fleury's carriage, and shouted and screamed at him, *du pain, du pain, du pain, nous mourons de faim*.

The old shoemaker earned what money he could, but life on the whole was hard in St. Nicaise, where in the narrow, dark and twisting streets, the drapers, the weavers and dyers earned their bread by hard labour, and only kept alive by sending their children out to work at an early age. Margaret Murphy, however, had other ideas for her children, and the hardworking, shrewd woman tramped the cobbled streets of Rouen peddling old clothes and toilet accessories. Despite the prevailing poverty and the harshness of life she insisted on dressing her daughters neatly and exploiting to the full the exquisite beauty of Marguerite and the attractive little Madeline who was already showing signs of acting ability. Margaret saw a great future for the two girls, and her mind naturally turned from provincial Rouen to Paris — the magnet for all France. There an opening might be found even for Brigitte, whose pock-marked face added to her plainness, but whose nimble and capable hands might be of some use, for she could ply a needle dexterously from her earliest years, and could also be employed at the bench of an artistic craft worker.

When Margaret Murphy first turned her thoughts to Paris her youngest child Victoire was six years old. She was a little brunette with a mass of ringlets haloing a pretty face, a mischievous upturned nose and sensuous pouting lips. She was still a little too fat for a child of her age, but she was a lively youngster. Though Margaret had set her heart on Paris there was no moving Daniel, who saw no reason for abandoning his trade and setting up elsewhere. God knew it was hard enough to make a living where he was without embarking on the hazards of a strange city where he knew nobody, and where it would be necessary to start life afresh — something very difficult for an old man.

In 1736, after a lapse of six years, Margaret Murphy was again pregnant. The baby born that autumn was another daughter and she was christened Marie Louise, the names of the Queen and the eldest daughter of Louis XV. Before very long the plump, fair, child promised to outdo her sisters

3

in good looks. Like most late children she was spoiled from the outset by an aged father, a doting mother and four older sisters, all petting and fondling her as though she was a little doll - a pretty plaything for all of them.

Two or three years after the birth of Louise (who was never called by her first name) Daniel Murphy died, leaving his widow and five daughters almost penniless. Fortunately the eldest of them had reached an age when she could help as a breadwinner. Margaret Murphy, however, was not one to sit down and bemoan her lot as if it was the end of the world and held no future for herself and her brood of daughters. Gathering together their few belongings, she brought her family to Paris, and there managed to find a couple of rooms in a tenement. Well used to the trade, and being a pushful and resourceful woman, she set up a stall as a second-hand clothes dealer in the Place du Palais Royal, around which revolved the life of the capital, the gay, the squalid, the sinful and the penitent — it was the microcosm of French life at its best, and also at its worst.

Paris, the *soi-disant* centre of the civilised world, offered a new life to Margaret Murphy, and even though she had only a stall from which to sell second-hand clothes, she saw around her the possibilities of a better life, a richer life for herself and her daughters in the shady world where a pretty girl could readily find a wealthy *roué* — a wife-tired nobleman, or some rich patron who was willing to set up a second establishment, and pay liberally for the pleasures of the flesh.

The Place du Palais Royal was a centre and meeting place for such marketeers, and the well-dressed, pretty, young ladies, and the aged shuffling *marcheuses* were all bent to the same purpose. Standing behind her stall it was soon clear to Margaret that the demand for young girls far exceeded the supply; this was particularly so in the case of attractive young women who could claim rightly or otherwise to have some background provided that it was not too tarnished, and they had an especial talent for entertaining the lecherous layabouts.

It is a little difficult to know how far Margaret Murphy was prepared to urge her daughters to look around for men willing to support them without necessarily contracting a marriage ceremony. After all, why should a pretty girl without means of any sort, with little in the nature of a home beyond ill-furnished rooms in a Paris slum, be condemned to pass her best years as a badly paid and overworked seamstress, or even as the wife of a workman who would only turn her into a drudge? Although she groomed her daughters for a future that was far from respectable, she never for a moment thought of them as common prostitutes or miserable streetwalkers likely to end their days in a lock hospital or even worse. Margaret was much too astute to encourage such a course or way of life, and before very long the dead cobbler of Rouen was completely forgotten and a new and more tangible image was born. Her late husband now assumed the posthumous role of a Jacobite exile, an Irish gentleman who had served in the armies of France; he was in fact of princely blood, — one of the O'Murphy's of Ballymore. He might very well have been an Irish gentleman, for the fortunes of war had stripped many Irishmen of all they possessed and forced them in the end to seek even the lowliest of trades. To a Murphy and a Hickey, however, these French-born girls owe a debt, for from their parents they inherited a certain natural charm, a light-hearted and devil-may-care gaiety, and the inexplicable poise and manner which is native to the Irish peasant.

At the age of fifteen, the good-humoured, gay and spritely Marguerite, with the approval and the blessing of her mother, was established in comfortable and neatly furnished rooms as the mistress of one Monsieur Meusiner who was a noted gambler, dandy, and man-about-town. Meusiner was an intimate friend and companion of Giacomo Casanova chevalier de Seingalt; he shared in many of his amours and escapades, and knew all the right people including Bachelier and Dominique-Guillaume Lebel, valets-de-chambre to Louis XV. Lebel, officially designated Concierge de Versailles, also combined the unpaid but recognised post of minister of the King's pleasures, and had entrance not only to the better known brothels of Paris, but behind stage in the theatres of Paris. Like Casanova he had a keen eye for a pretty girl, particularly if she was unused by other men, for at this period he drew the line at foisting common grisettes on his Majesty whose taste in this regard was not yet fully debased; at this period he preferred virgins or newly deflowered girls.

With Marguerite off her hands, nicely established, and no doubt contributing a little money to the household, Madame O'Morphi, as she now was, turned her attention to Brigitte who was almost fourteen years old. Unfortunately Brigitte was not quite so desirable or acceptable to a wealthy and pleasure-seeking client as her pretty sister; her somewhat plain and pocked features militated against her, and while Madame O'Morphi was not particularly scrupulous or God-fearing, she would not have her daughter consigned to the brothels which abounded in the labyrinth of narrow streets and alleys off the Place du Palais Royal, even those used by a better class of client.

Brigitte's capable hands helped her to some extent, for she was a creative youngster, and her nimble fingers could be turned to some practical purpose. In due course, therefore, she was employed as a maker of false pearls in a rather shady establishment. Somewhat later she was able to supplement her wages by occasional employment as an artist's model, particularly as a model for hands. In this way she found a niche in the mid-world of art and harlotry.

The newly established clothes dealer in the Place du Palais Royal was not doing too badly; indeed, Madame O'Morphi was more than capable of holding her own with the hard-headed dealers and shopkeepers thronging this area. The truth, however, would seem to be that the selling and buying of old clothes was simply a respectable façade which enabled Madame O'Morphi to pursue the more rewarding and lucrative avocation of procuress, obtaining girls to fill a role for which there was apparently an insatiable demand, despite the fact that the Palais Royal quarter had many hundred 'filles' — in fact one to every seventy inhabitants of the city. A police dossier still exists which would suggest that Margaret O'Morphi was a Madame and procuress, and this avocation, by no means dishonourable or frowned upon in eighteenth century France, enabled her to choose, when she so wished, the richer and more reputable clients for her daughters; clients who were at least prepared to set up homes for them and pay well for the privilege of enjoying what they had to offer.

The growth, development and popularity of the theatre in Paris, which was enthusiastically encouraged during the reign of Louis XV, despite the monopolistic opposition of the Comédie Francaise, provided a new and alluring opening for pretty girls, more particularly if they were pleasant and could sing, mime, and dance.

The Opéra-Comique which was founded about 1724 at the Foire St. Laurent offered such an opportunity during its brief lifetime. The managers, actors and playwrights connected with it were on the whole a strange lot of people. The first manager was an ex-tallow chandler who obtained a licence to direct it for three years. He was later replaced by a dissolute and dissipated actor named Boizard de Portau whose assistant was a rather disreputable individual named Meyer but commonly called Devienne. Then there was Favart, the son of a jovial pastrycook, who learned rhymes and tunes from his father, 'and while the father had been content to let his rhymes go with the wind, the son strung his together and made little plays of them'. Some of the foremost French writers supplied the Opéra-Comique with material, and such names as Prion, Le Sage, Fuzélier and Dorneval were commonplace among the contributors. Panard, a big genial drunkard, whose outsize glass held a bottleful of wine wrote more than eight plays for it.

About the time the O'Morphi girls appeared upon the scene, Favart had given up the management of the Opéra-Comique and the new licensee was the unscrupulous and cunning Jean Monet. One of the first things Monet did was to repair and rebuild the theatre, and also a second one close by at the Foire St. Germain. Both theatres when acquired were in a lamentable condition. When the theatres were repaired, Monet gathered together an excellent company and recruited a host of pretty young dancers. Besides the actors and the dancers, he sought the advice of the painter Boucher, and employed a number of art students to paint scenery. As a result of his enterprise a period of prosperity seemed to be in store for him and the public flocked to his theatre. This success was Monet's undoing. As soon as the Opéra-Comique appeared to be doing well and achieving a substantial measure of success the directors of the Comédie Francaise stepped in and claimed that as the State theatre it had the sole right to use dialogue. Monet threw in the sponge, and in 1744 Favart again took control and the Opéra-Comique became the home of the pantomime and light opera.

Madeline, perhaps the most attractive and certainly the most intelligent of Madame O'Morphi's daughters, was readily accepted as an actress at the Opéra-Comique. Here the young girl with her good looks, her slim figure and her gay and talented vivacity, her dancing, singing and miming attracted considerable attention. She gathered a number of young men about her with whom she had numerous love affairs; they no doubt were attracted by her good looks and her lighthearted gaiety. In time she established a salon of sorts to which the wealthy *roués* had access, and to add respectability to her actions, she married an amiable actor named Corbier who closed an eye to her extra-marital activities and her free and easy life — but then Corbier had no reason to complain for he was a much married man and now past his prime.

Madeline's younger sister Victoire, growing up in this atmosphere of amorality and lechery, matured quickly and precociously, and showed every promise of real beauty. At the age of thirteen a protector had been found for her. This was President St. Lubin of the Parlement of France, who at first apprenticed her to a picture dealer in the Place du Vieux Louvre, and paid him well for her board and keep. However, after the lapse of some months, and as Victoire was showing signs of early puberty and precociousness, he placed her in a convent, hoping to keep her there until such time as she was sufficiently mature for his personal use. The abnormal precocity of the O'Morphi girls was something St. Lubin overlooked, believing as he did that strict confinement behind high convent walls and under the care of good and holy nuns was the only certain way of safeguarding the virginity of his mistress-to-be. Boccaccio's tales of an earlier century fitted closely to the Paris of the Regency and the days of Louis XV, when convents offered neither insurance for purity nor a safety belt for the chaste.

Some months before the patient but eager St. Lubin could enjoy the fruits of his abstinence, Victoire gave birth to a child, and to add insult to injury it would seem, on well authenticated grounds, that this love-child was fathered by St. Lubin's young nephew, a spry young man who knew quite a lot about his uncle's affairs and was fond of pretty girls. Despite the moral weakness or the insatiable proclivity of the O'Morphi clan, there is no doubt that they were a tightly knit family and very loyal to one another at all times; this statement is borne out by the fact that Victoire's child was born in Madeline's home and was actually christened Madeline.

Whatever his first feelings may have been, M. le President overlooked the lapse of his young protégé and again took her under his wing and enjoyed the pleasures the pretty brunette offered him. Shortly after setting Victoire up in pleasant rooms of her own, St. Lubin established the Theatre Flamand under the assumed ownership of St. Gratien and gave Victoire her first experience of the stage. The Theatre Flamand did not last very long and a year or two later, Victoire appeared as a dancer at the popular Opéra-Comique. It was at this theatre, with its large troop of pretty young dancers, she first attracted the attention of the then fashionable and popular artist François Boucher, whose erotic and sensuous work was the rage of Paris. Boucher was later to become the protégé and favourite painter of the Marquise de Pompadour whose portrait he had often painted, and he decorated the rooms of her palaces with lively and voluptuous scenes which she knew would give fresh heart to her royal paramour and titillate his gross sensual appetite.

Boucher had a genuine artist's eye for beauty and shapeliness and, being always fond of pretty, young women who were willing to play a dual role in his atelier, engaged Victoire as a model. From the outset he found she was a good-natured girl with a piquant sense of humour and a certain light-hearted gaiety. Though well versed in the ways of the world, Victoire could be pleasingly unsophisticated, and this unsophistication was part of the ordinary, almost simple, child-like, naturalness which was characteristic of all the O'Morphi girls. They willingly accepted amorality as a pleasant and easy way of life and they seemed to have enjoyed it.

L'Odalisque (*Victoire O'Murphi*), (*Musée des Beaux-Arts, Reims*).

The Painter of Paris

When Victoire O'Morphi first attracted the attention of Boucher he was in his early forties. As a painter and voluptuary he was all the rage of Paris. His paintings with their curious eroticism and profusion of pink-tinted nudes — warm and nubile — were readily sought after, and adorned the homes of many of the more profligate nobles of Paris, particularly those whose virility had declined and required the titillation which Boucher's paintings evoked.

François Boucher — man and artist — epitomised the France of his day, or to be more precise the Paris of his day — a gay, pleasure-loving and completely amoral city. He was born in the shadow of the Louvre in the year 1703, a year of many disasters, and one marking the declining power of Louis XIV, *le Roi Soleil*. It was a time when a great nation was virtually on its knees begging mercy from numerous enemies, and striving to regain some of its former greatness in the face of adversity. The nation's coffers were empty and so were the stomachs of the populace. In spite of poverty, internecine strife, and a general malaise, the splendour and extravagance of the French court remained undiminished, and its moral tone was that of one vast seraglio.

Boucher's father belonged to the *petite bourgeoisie*, and kept a small shop where he sold designs, drawings, engraving and paintings at a low price. Though a poor designer and little favoured by fortune he encouraged the evident artistic skill of his son, and taught him the rudiments of drawing and painting. Old man Boucher had faith in his son's capabilities and devoted a considerable time to his artistic training with the avowed intention of placing him in the studio of one or other of the notable teachers of the day when he was old enough, and had acquired sufficient practical knowledge to work with a master.

The steep slide into a world of decadence and turpitude was accelerated in France after the death of Louis XIV in 1715, and the accession of a Council of Regency under the dissolute Duc D'Orléans during the minority of the Dauphin. A carnival of fun, of luxury, of unlicensed and unbridled pleasure was virtually inaugurated by the Duc d'Orléans; the disciplining virtues were lightly regarded, if regarded at all, and the demimondes of the city moved up into society like an invading army or a plague of locusts. The Church, the Court, *la haute société*, the *petite bourgeoisie* and even the lower orders were tarred with the same brush; it was an age of deliberate profligacy and few decried it. The Vicomte de Bros, an interesting spectator, wrote: 'The licentiousness of the Regency had made the gallantry of the Court of Louis XIV degenerate into a frantic libertinism. Marriage was looked upon as an institution useful for increasing fortunes and providing heirs for a family and establishments for daughters, but only made supportable by avoiding all its duties and restraints.'

Of course the Court of Louis XIV was not without its periods of moral turpitude and the King in the earlier years of his reign accepted the favours of humble women, including peasant wenches, gardeners' daughters and chambermaids as well as notables such as Madame de Montespan and Madame de Maintenon. It is claimed that he sired no less than nine illegitimate children. His brother too was a noted *roué* who in outbursts of religious zeal and contrition rubbed a holy medal over his naked body. This action did not pass unnoticed by his wife who once told him, 'You cannot convince me that you are honouring the Virgin Mary by promenading her image over those parts which are destined to put an end to virginity.'

The regency of Philippe d'Orléans is stigmatised as a period when morality was at its lowest ebb. It was an era of profligacy and no attempt was made to conceal it. Little wonder therefore that Margaret Murphy, even though her daughters were still children, saw a bright future not only for them when they reached the age of puberty, but even for herself in middle age if she employed the cunning subtlety so much part of her Irish heritage. However, so far as she was concerned this was still somewhat in the future but it was the world in which the young Boucher grew to manhood and in which the boy-King gained early experience. Boucher, even as a young man with scarcely a *sou* in his pocket did not escape from the prevailing atmosphere of his native city. As an impoverished student he enjoyed the license that captivated all classes of society and he prided himself in his knowledge of the fair sex and all their wiles.

At the age of seventeen, Boucher became a pupil in the studio of François Lemoyne, then at his height of his fame as a painter in the style

11

of Le Brun and whose unique decorations at Versailles brought him fame. Though Lemoyne was a relatively young man and a favourite at the court of the Duc d'Orléans he would appear to have had little time to give to the many students he undertook to teach. Young Boucher spent only about three months in his master's atelier, but these months were apparently well spent.

While still a student with Lemoyne, Boucher completed a large and sumptuous canvas 'Le Jugement de Susanne' which won the praise and approval of his master, and this encouraged him to work on still larger canvases covered with highly decorative figures scattered in profusion over his massive works. These large paintings took time however, so in order to provide the bread and butter to enable him to paint in the grand style, he went to live with the engraver Cars for whom he worked in return for board and lodgings and sixty livres a month pocket money. Cars was a popular engraver and Boucher helped him by devising tailpieces and orna-mental devices for books. Working hard under his new master he soon became an engraver of some ability, and in time was put to work engraving a number of Watteau's sensuous and delicate drawings which undoubtedly affected his style, and inspired him to some extent.

About this time Boucher was introduced as a promising and competent, young painter to the proprietors of the new Opéra-Comique which had just been built at the Foire St. Laurent and was run by Maurice Honoré who though an ex-tallow chandler had a warm love of the theatre. This introduction led to Boucher's employment as a scene painter, a somewhat laborious and tedious task and not very highly regarded. Nevertheless this kind of work was much sought after, and was most acceptable to young artists, not only for the money which they earned, but the opportunity it gave to work quickly and expertly on huge canvases and with unlimited supplies of paint and brushes. Scene painting, and particularly at the Opéra-Comique, lent itself to vast, imaginative, if somewhat unreal work; and the use of colour to brighten the stage, ill-illuminated at the time, required a flair and imaginative sense of light and shade in which the young Boucher revelled.

With free and complete entry to the theatre, Boucher found himself among a group of young and lively people who satisfied to the full his growing sensuality. At the Opéra-Comique he met and was joined by another young artist, Carl van Loo, who was a year or two younger, but was already showing considerable talent and maturity as a decorative artist. Soon the two young men were working together, virtually monopolising all the scene painting in the theatre, and were executing large canvases with

12

scenes highly evocative of the libertinism of the age and enhancing the provocative nature of the dances.

The *milieu* of the Opéra-Comique suited the pleasure-seeking Boucher who, when necessary, worked hard and for long hours, but at the same time took his pleasures with equal verve and enthusiasm. In this regard he was no better and no worse than the majority of Parisians. The ebullient and warm-blooded, young artist carried on one liaison after another with the pretty, young actresses and ballet girls who found an exciting career in this new theatre, particularly when it came under the management of the witty but dissipated actor Boizard de Portau and his dubious assistant Devienne. Boucher revelled in the wild and unrestrained back-stage parties, and glowed in the *soi-disant* salons set up by some of the leading actors and actresses. Thus even as a youth his 'character and art were tainted with the vice and corruption of the Regency'.

Though a somewhat dissolute and dissipated young man, Boucher worked hard not only for his engraver friend Laurent Cars for whom he did an immense number of exquisite designs and illustrations, but also at the Opéra-Comique where he had become the leading scene painter. Though engraving and scene painting took up quite a lot of his time, the young artist did not neglect the work he really loved, and during these years of apprenticeship, he submitted a number of paintings to the Académie Royale de Peinture et de Sculpture. In 1723, when he was only twenty, Boucher received the Premier Grand Prix de Peinture for a canvas depicting Merodach delivering Joash from chains, the subject set by the judges for the award. This much coveted prize entitled the recipient to free board and lodgings, and a pension of three hundred livres while studying at the Académie.

With pension and board, Boucher was now freed from the necessity of wasting his ability painting scenes for the theatre, scenes which, though requiring skill, did not exact detailed execution, nor was it necessary to spend long hours in Cars' workshop. He had time now to devote his energy and ability to painting under skilled masters at the Académie. In the course of the next year or two his name began to be known outside the narrow circle of his masters and fellow-pupils and the pretty little grisettes who earned a pittance as models. Patrons began to appear from the nobility and well-to-do classes, including the well known collector and patron Baron de Thiers who commissioned Boucher to do a number of paintings for his country house.

The patronage and encouragement of individuals like the Baron de Thiers had an astonishing effect on the young artist, who for the next few years worked with untiring energy and extraordinary facility, caring less for profit from his paintings than acquiring a reputation as a skilful artist. His first canvas of merit on the grand scale to evoke and excite public admiration and measure of praise was the 'Enlèvement d'Europe'. This painting, alive with imaginative beauty and grave sensuality, was evocative of Boucher's art and executed in a genre typical of his later work. In this work the plump cherubs and well-rounded nubile girls shocked the austere and prudish but were acclaimed by the pleasure-loving Parisians always looking for something new and sensational.

Boucher's intimate acquaintance with the dainty ballerinas and the appetent grisettes gave him an abundance of delightful models with which to fill every inch of his canvases and he revelled in this. Soon his studio began to resemble a bordel stacked with erotic and sensual paintings, paintings such as 'L'Amour moisonneur', 'L'Amour oiseleur' and 'L'Amour vendangeur' which were typical of his work at this time. These paintings were vividly alive with a sensuous beauty of their own; they were imaginative and provocative to a degree unattained by his contemporaries and had a parallel in the literary achievement of Casanova.

Boucher was undoubtedly filling a demand in producing canvases of an erotic nature which were sought after by the engravers who had a limitless market for pictures of this sort. He was earning a lot of money and acquiring a notoriety for eroticism. Suddenly, like other voluptuaries, he was smitten by remorse and became for a time truly penitent. In this mood he destroyed some of his more lascivious pictures, turned less sensuous ones to the walls of his studio, and commenced to paint, not successfully, a series of religious and allegorical pictures mainly based on biblical stories. He locked himself in his studio and hermit-like cut himself adrift from the gay and sensual world which had inspired him. It was said that when one of his wealthiest patrons, the Comte de Caylus asked, 'Que fais-tu donc?' he replied sorrowfully, 'Je fais pénitence.' .

After three weeks of seclusion, Boucher left his hideout, and passing by a fruit shop where he stopped to make a purchase, he was struck by the innocent beauty of a young girl serving behind the fruit-laden counter. The young girl who was called Rosine stood before him with pink, bare arms, and loose black hair falling about her shoulders; her soft, smiling face shone with a child-like innocence that captivated the artist, and for the first time he beheld what he conceived vaguely in his mind to be the likeness of the Blessed Virgin Mary. Somewhat diffidently and with little of the brashness he usually displayed with the opposite sex, he asked Rosine if she would pose for some paintings he was doing. The virginal Rosine was doubtful; models were, in her mind, depraved creatures, little better than harlots, utterly shameless in the naked exposure of their bodies. But her mother, with true Parisian realism, answered for her, and the next morning she brought her blushing and protesting daughter to Boucher's atelier.

Boucher immediately commenced work on a new picture of the Blessed Virgin, a picture tinged with idealism but taken from life. He was enraptured with his young model, and his gaze wandered more often to Rosine than to the slowly developing figure on his canvas. After a few days of this Boucher was more his old self. Rosine was no longer just a model sitting coldly, impersonally, by his easel, but a beautiful young woman who could be fondled and loved, and Boucher was not slow in making known his desires. Innocent, shy and romantic, Rosine's resistance was half-hearted. She knew nothing much about Boucher except that he was a handsome young man, an artist, and that he said he loved her. Perhaps he did, but her conception of love was something more romantic and lasting than his. She was ignorant of the fleeting nature of his passions, ignorant and innocent, assuming that love was something idyllic and lasted for ever. But to Boucher, particularly at this stage of his life, love was little more than a passing whim, something to be enjoyed, tasted and forgotten and this was understood by the ballet girls and young actresses of the Opéra-Comique, the grisettes, the erstwhile models and prostitutes who thronged the artists' studios, walked the narrow streets or exposed and displayed their charms behind the basement grills in the lanes of St. Eustache, St. Merri and the much better known and frequented establishments or bordels in the Rue de Venise.

A period of intense industry and idyllic love-making ensued and Rosine was happy. But like so much in life the dream ended and Rosine found herself supplanted and cast aside. The records claim she died of a broken heart. All this of course happened before the O'Morphi girls graced the studio of a mature and well-established Boucher, and though the pattern was very much the same the O'Morphi girls as we shall see were not quite as expendable as simple grisettes.

It was shortly after this that Boucher, availing himself of the Prix de Rome, which he was awarded, decided to go to Italy. He was about twenty-four years old at the time, a gay, charming, light-hearted, young man, fond of wine and women, and of all the other good things of life. He was accompanied by Carle van Loo who was his very opposite in most things. Carle had no interest in the gay, uninhibited, life which Boucher loved and lived. On the contrary he had inherited the slow, stolid, almost ponderous, nature of his Flemish grandfather. He worked very hard and methodically, and though in the course of time he became a fine painter, he was never more than a really competent craftsman, who painted just what he saw, exactly as he saw it, and did not permit his imagination to run riot, and conjure the great imaginative pictures of his contemporaries.

In Rome the two young men dutifully visited the galleries and the palaces and homes where the Old Masters were to be seen, but Boucher, rather full of his own importance had little time for the Old Masters; he had all the critical rebelliousness and assumed knowledge of youth, and could see little good in the works of the dead. Raphael was *fade*, Michael Angelo *bossu*, and what he thought of other Masters of the past has not been recorded. However, there was one Italian contemporary painter, then at the height of his fame, he really admired, and whose work won his approval and appreciation. That was Tiepolo, the last of the really great Venetian decorators, and still the finest exponent of Italian rococo. Tiepolo, though at the height of his fame, was only seven or eight years older than Boucher, and had just completed his brilliant and superb decorations at the Udine Palace, a task which had taken him three years to complete. Tiepolo was of course a brilliant and expert craftsman, a man wholly dedicated to his art who worked long and weary hours with a number of young artists and students who were similarly dedicated to their work and who religiously carried out their master's instructions and teaching.

The young Boucher formed a friendship with Tiepolo; indeed it is thought that he may have been for a short time one of his assistants and worked with him at the Udine Palace. Certainly the brash, young artist was impressed by the grand manner and the extravagance of the master and Tiepolo undoubtedly influenced him in later life. The head of the Academy at Rome also took an interest in Boucher. In fact the young man was always very popular and made friends easily. In due course he was provided with a small studio and when not holding some riotous party — a bacchanalian feast — and sleeping off the effects, he worked hard and painted a number of pictures, many of a religious nature, for these were much sought after to decorate the innumerable churches, chapels, convents and religious houses abounding in Italy, which unlike his native France still venerated and prized religious works of one sort or another. Among his more notable pictures at this period were 'Le Départ de Joseph, entrant dans l'Arche', 'Rencontre de Jacob et de Rachel', 'Mariage des Enfants de Dieu avec les Enfants des Hommes'.

Boucher remained in Rome for about three years, and while there is little known about his life there, Arsène Houssaye records that 'he lived in extravagant dissipation, and gave a splendid fête in which everyone appeared as a mythological character, he himself being disguised as Jupiter'. This party or feast would appear to have been his farewell to Rome, for he returned to Paris in 1731, still unimpressed by the Old Masters — with the possible exception of Paolo Veronese, whose paintings of biblical and allegorical figures and scenes crowded with golden-haired maidens, courtiers, musicians and splendidly ornate soldiers appealed to his taste and stirred his imagination. Of course during his sojourn in Italy he absorbed every detail of the superb rococo art of Tiepolo; this great master became his mentor, and he closely followed his style in later years. Though he may have been extremely critical of what he had seen in Rome, in a brash self-opinionated way, there is not the slightest doubt that the vast canvases, with their superb detail and richness of colour, contributed to Boucher's understanding of art; he could not but absorb something of what he had seen, and this helped to make him the most typical if not the most skilful artist of the later French rococo.

The Paris to which Boucher returned had changed very little since his departure. The young Dauphin had been crowned King of France. His uncle, the worldly, bawdy, and licentious Regent, the Duc d'Orléans had died, leaving behind him a legacy of dissolution almost unparalleled in contemporary Europe. Liselotte records of him: 'He was quite crazy about women, provided they were good-tempered, indelicate, great eaters and drinkers; he troubled little about their looks'. When Liselotte chided him for his uncritical choice of gross and ugly women he blandly replied: 'Bah! Maman, la nuit tous les chats son gris.' Liselotte might have added, though the Duc d'Orléans was not particular in his choice of women, they in turn, from the noblest in the land, begged the privilege of sharing his bed. With all his faults, however, the Regent was a man of liberal ideas, he was a lover of the arts, a brave and gallant soldier and we may assume that many of his attributed debaucheries were the boastings of a man who loved to shock others and boastfully emulate those whom he called 'mes roués'. Somebody or other wrote that he had the artistic temperament of a Renaissance Prince but the morals of a tomcat. He died at the age of forty-nine exhausted by his sexual excesses, an impotent libertine reduced to voyeurism at the orgies he hosted.

Maria-Jeanne

When Margaret Murphy brought her five daughters to Paris and set up her stall in the Place du Palais Royal, Louis XV was a young man of twenty-eight. He was a slim, handsome man and evinced little interest in anything but hunting, which to him was not just a diversion and healthy sport, but an absorbing passion. Except for hunting the young King lived a life of idleness, delegating all power and authority to Cardinal de Fleury, who as Bishop of Fréjus had undertaken the care and education of the boy-king. As first minister and the absolute power behind the throne, Cardinal de Fleury was a marked contrast to the Duc d'Orléans. He preferred sound economy to glory, and worked hard to stabilize the finances of the country which had been in a deplorable condition. In private life he lived rather simply, he scorned all opportunity to enrich himself, and sought only the glory and greatness of his beloved France. After the warring years of Louis XIV, and the wild extravagance of the Regency, the more solid rule of the Cardinal was a relief. Fleury's reign of seventeen years was a time of peace abroad, economy at home, and a decided reformation in court life. Ministers and members of the court entourage undoubtedly continued to keep mistresses and sought lovers, but they kept them very much in the background and never flaunted them with the undisguised blatancy of the Regency.

The King's life of idleness which bred eventual boredom was not greatly helped by the general background of his private life. He was a mere boy of sixteen when he married Marie Leczinska, the daughter of the deposed king, Stanislas of Poland. She was twenty-three years old at the time of her betrothal; she was not beautiful by comparison with many of the court ladies; but she was pleasant looking, attractive in her gentle ways, fairly intelligent and tactful. These attributes served her well for a short time. But Louis never really cared for her, and she simply served the purpose of bearing children to ensure the continuance of the monarchy. Even then her luck did not hold out for it was only after a succession of daughters that a Dauphin was born, and one son was but a slender thread to assure succession to the throne of France. Still the birth of a single son was sufficient excuse for the king to visit the bed-chamber less frequently, though he did keep the queen in a perpetual state of pregnancy which constrained her to remark bitterly: 'Toujours coucher, toujours grossesse, toujours accoucher'.

Worn out with child-bearing, seven years older than her husband, very prudish and excessively boring, she made little or no effort to hold the king or retain what little affection he had for her in the face of the advances of such women of the world as his cousin de Charolais, the Comtesse de Toulouse, and the Comtesse de Vintimille. Thus from about the year 1738, the King ceased to sleep with his wife, his action being attributed in the main to her refusal to receive him after a *fausse couche*, as she had been told by her doctors that another pregnancy might be dangerous, and that some little time should elapse before she slept with her husband again. Very stupidly she kept this information from the King, and simply refused to receive him in bed.

While the widowed Margaret Murphy struggled hard to maintain herself and her young children, François Boucher, who was not even a name to her at the time, but who perhaps more than anybody else brought eventual fame and notoriety to at least two of her daughters, was well launched on his career as the premier painter of France. He was now producing massive and superb works redolent of the influence of Tiepolo and Veronese. His years in Rome had not been wasted and this was evident in such paintings as 'Vénus commandant à Vulcan les armes d'Enée'. 'La Naissance', and 'La Mort d'Adonis'. Boucher worked with a new and beautiful model to whom he was much attached. She was slight, very fair, almost golden-haired; furthermore she was gay and light-hearted, vivacious, with smiling blue eyes; a little goddess almost. She was Maria Jeanne Buseaux, the daughter of a fairly well-to-do middle class family living in the rue du Temple. She was only seventeen years old when Boucher met her, but 'her surpassing beauty made her of inestimable value as a model, and far outweighed her want of fortune'. The sophisticated Boucher fell hopelessly in love with her; there was no question of seduction, for no sooner had she sat for him than he proposed the marriage which took place in the church of Saint Roch on the 21st April 1733, and the young couple settled down in a

19

Boucher with his wife and children about 1739 (Musée du Louvre, Paris)

house in the rue Saint Thomas du Louvre, where they were to live for the next ten years.

Maria Jeanne filled a new role in her husband's life and growing achievement. She was in the first place a lively, intellectual companion; she was very fond of him, and for at least the early years of their marriage faithful to him, despite a considerable disparity in ages. She was artistic, interested in his work and of help to him. She translated into bronze some of his ideas and made a number of miniatures of his pictures; she was of even more benefit as his model, perhaps his favourite model. From the very first day he met her, he painted her over and over again as a charming shepherdess, a delightful nymph, and a goddess without compare. She filled the role so completely that her figure was indelibly implanted in his mind, the figure of the slender, beautiful young bride so 'that she triumphs in the works of the master through the years'.

A study of Boucher's paintings shows clearly the role played by his wife. Picture after picture depicts her grace, her loveliness, her beauty. 'She sits as on a throne, on a seashell amid the nereids in the ''Triumph of Venus'' under the long scarf of striped silk which unfurls in the sky. She is receiving pearls which are being offered to her by a nymph up-lifted by the strong arms of a triton. Her young, firm, breasts catch the light which in turn trickles down her lithe and slim body. Her tiny face, under her short, blonde, hair, has an amused expression; her eyes smiling under half lowered lids.' We see her again with the same roguish air, the same slim and perfect body in 'Leda' and many similar pictures. In a note penned many years later in *Le Nécrologe*, the writer says: 'We cannot let it be unknown that having had, like Albane, the happiness to choose a companion who was able to communicate, without ceasing, her lovely grace, he knew, like a great man, how best to use this for his art.'

Though now the wife of a painter of considerable eminence, and undoubted charm, Maria Jeanne 'savait sans doute ne pouvoir compter longtemps sur la constance de son époux'. He was much sought after; he was flattered and loved by the beautiful and dissolute Duchesse d'Orléans. Maria Jeanne was not greatly perturbed by her husband's infidelities; there was a kind of understanding between them and she had nothing to fear, certainly not the innumerable tarts, grisettes and models filing through his studio; they were for the most part ignorant, stupid little things earning a pittance to assuage their hunger. Some perhaps became passing fancies and Boucher enjoyed them, but for the most part they meant nothing to him beyond being voluptuous figures to fill the lush canvases he painted with tremendous élan. By contrast Maria Jeanne suited Boucher admirably, and

Madame Boucher about 1745 (A Mme Hecter Petin, Paris)

besides acting as a model, caring for their children, she had considerable taste and talent herself. Because of her beauty she was eagerly sought after by other artists; perhaps the most charming and delightful portrait of her was that exhibited in the salon of 1737, and painted by Maurice de la Tour, the most celebrated French pastellist of the eighteenth century. She was also painted in later years by Roslin, the Swedish portrait painter who spent many years in Paris, but the finest tribute to the beauty of Maria Jeanne is to be seen in Boucher's painting 'Renaud et Armid', in the Louvre. Perhaps the best compliment to her beauty were the words attributed to Boucher's friend Bachaumont, who, when consulted as to what subjects the artist should choose for a series of pictures to illustrate the fable of *Psyche*, replied: 'Read and read again the *Psyche* of La Fontaine, and above all things study well Madame Boucher.'

In 1734, Boucher was formally declared an Academician, and for the occasion of his election painted 'Renaud et Armid'. This painting, so unlike anything he had hitherto done, enhanced his reputation. Success followed success, and commissions poured into the studio. He became the delineator of the dissolute Paris of his day; his gay and faintly erotic flesh-tinted paintings were eagerly sought after and new ones commissioned to enhance the houses of the nobility. Shortly after his election to the Academy, Boucher received his first commission from the young King who had not yet abandoned his wife and embarked on his amoral career. Boucher was asked to decorate the Queen's bedroom with paintings of a more cheerful and lively nature than the faded and uninteresting pictures decorating the walls for many years.

The opening of the Paris Salon in 1737, after a lapse of more than thirty years, was an event in the artistic world, and marked a turning point in Boucher's career. For the occasion he exhibited six large paintings, four pastorals, and two ovals representing the seasons which had been commissioned by the young King. About this time too, the Prince de Soubise, a favourite of the King and later Marshal of France, began the construction of the Hôtel de Soubise which in the course of a few years became one of the most beautiful palaces in Paris, displaying the exquisite charm which French art attained in the middle of the eighteenth century. For this task he chose Boucher and his friend Carle van Loo to decorate the rooms. Boucher did seven erotic paintings for the building, 'Les Trois Grâces que enchaînent l'Amour', 'L'Education de L'Amour par Mercure', 'L'Amour et Céphale', 'Vénus appuyant sur Cupidon pour entrer au bain en descendant de sa chaire', 'Vénus et L'Amour', and two paintings of a shepherd and shepherdess.

About the same time as Boucher was completing his paintings for the Paris Salon, Oudry had taken over the conduct of the famous Beauvais factories and engaged Boucher to provide designs for the beautiful tapestries he produced, designs whose original and fresh style, colour and arrangements increased the reputation and the products of the famous looms. Among the most notable paintings executed for this purpose were 'Bacchus et Ariadne', 'La Bonne Aventure', and the well known 'Fountain of Love'.

Boucher was now in the top flight of French artists, immensely popular and eagerly sought after. He was a welcome guest in Madame Geoffrin's salon. She had been a good friend and patron when he was a younger man, and purchased his 'Aurora et Thétis' when he was less well known. It was at Madame Geoffrin's salon that Boucher had the good fortune to be introduced by Charles Le Normand de Tournehem to a delightful and beautiful young lady, Le Normand d'Étiolles. Charles did not tell Boucher that he was the father of the young lady who was as delicate as a piece of Dresden, but simply spoke of her as his niece. Her real name was Jeanne-Antoinette Poisson, the daughter of the beautiful wife of Monsieur Poisson who had been cuckold. Though Boucher knew the young lady was married, he did not know that the husband (who was kept very much in the background and whose name was rarely mentioned) was in fact a nephew of M. Charles Le Normand. He was very rich, and a rather plain and inconsequential young man but deeply in love with Toinette. Toinette, a ravishing twenty-one year old, spent very little time with her meek and adoring husband, but she was much sought after at Madame Geoffrin's salon, and men hung round her like wasps on a jam dish.

In time the lively and vivacious Toinette had a minor salon of her own, a salon which was frequented by Voltaire, Fontenelle, Crébillon and other literati, as well as the ever-popular Boucher. Toinette's salon had more of the warm and friendly intimacy of a large family circle than a salon, and 'uncle' Tournehem who so skilfully arranged the marriage of his daughter and nephew, built the beautiful château d'Étiolles for the young couple, and saw that the house was worthy of a young lady who would, in time, become the most powerful woman in France. A small theatre was constructed in the house, and Toinette, now on fairly intimate terms with Boucher, asked him to design and decorate it, which he was delighted to do.

In her splendid home, Toinette was the hostess *par excellence*, and the guests enjoyed luscious repasts, including game from the Royal preserves, for the King had caught a fleeting glimpse of the beautiful Toinette, and much to the envy of his current mistress, the Duchesse de Châteauroux, ordered that some of the fruits of the Royal hunt be delivered to the Château d'Étiolles for the delectation and enjoyment of Toinette and her guests.

Boucher's introduction to Madame Le Normand d'Etiolles marked another milestone on the road to success, but even he could not foresee that his lovely, young patron would in a few years be the all-powerful Marquise de Pompadour, and would overwhelm him with commissions and other marks of favour, which would place him in the front rank of French arists.

The Pompadour

The years rolled rapidly by. Louis XV had completely abandoned his love-less Queen for a succession of noble mistresses who satisfied his abnormal sexual appetite, and a few grisettes to pander to his carnal instincts. The painter Boucher was now accepted as the most fasionable painter in all France, with an elegant and eager clientele clamouring for his most sensual and erotic paintings. For some years now his lovely wife had served him well as a model, but as the mother of two growing daughters and a young son she could no longer compete with the galaxy of young nudes extravagantly filling every inch of his exciting canvases, and the insistent demand for more sumptuous and sensual paintings constrained him to seek new and more nubile models.

In the meantime the O'Morphi girls, now delightful young women of the world were fulfilling their predestined roles as superior odalisques. Marguerite, the eldest of the family, had dropped her first wealthy patron, the lawyer Meusnier, and concealed her well paid activities under the respectable name of Madame Melun. With the approval and support of her mother she had introduced the pock-marked and rather plain Brigitte into the exciting world of the demi-monde. Marguerite, always blessed with unusual vivacity and *joie de vivre,* had quite a large circle of friends in many places, and with their aid and influence she was able to help Brigitte gain entry to the Academy as a *modéle en titre,* something above the average model brought in from the street when required. Brigitte continued to work in the Academy for a number of years, and very possibly endures an anonymous immortality in the early works of artists who later achieved fame.

Though Boucher no longer painted scenes for the Opéra-Comique he was a fairly constant visitor backstage. He found the pretty little dancers and singers not only entertaining in their own way, but he derived enjoyment from the somewhat unconventional and light-hearted life of the theatre, and at this time, though married and a father, he was a 'gay, somewhat dissipated devil-may-care dandy of a man, handsomely dressed, smiling out of his careless day'. Moving among the young dancers one day, Boucher's eyes and fancy rested on the pretty and vivacious Victoire O'Morphi. The lovely brunette was fourteen or fifteen years old when Boucher first met her, and though little more than a child in years she was well versed in the ways of life and love, for old Margaret O'Morphi never believed in spoiling her children or standing in the way of their social advancement; in fact she encouraged them.

About the time Boucher first showed an interest in Victoire, he had moved into a house in the rue de Grenelle, which he furnished in a grand and sumptuous style. He had an atelier in the house and also a studio and rooms in the Louvre, where a number of young painters had attached themselves to him. It is a little difficult to know what the artist's exact relations were with Victoire, though there is no doubt he was sufficiently attracted to the young girl, with the perfectly formed body, the small round breasts, the sensuous mouth and gay, sparkling eyes, to invite her to his studio. Very shortly after this initial meeting he engaged her as his *modèle en titre*; in other words chief or principal model.

It is not always easy to identify Victoire in Boucher's paintings owing to the fact that the date of some of these paintings is obscure, and the features of the model often resemble Jeanne Boucher in her more youthful days. The most notable painting of Boucher's and certainly executed about the time Victoire was a model is the well-known 'L'Odalisque'. This erotic and exciting picture created quite a stir when it was first exhibited, and though well received and warmly praised by the pleasure-loving Parisians, it was strongly condemned by Diderot and others as a sign of the decadence of French art.

'L'Odalisque' has been the subject of controversy for more than two hundred years, and a number of names have been suggested and put forward as the actual model. The controversy stems in the main from the fact that the exact date of the painting is not very clear. The painting is dated 174?, the last year being undecipherable, and is variously fixed between 1742 and 1748. Accepting either the earliest or latest date some of the models mentioned can be readily eliminated. It has been claimed, by one authority that the model was Madame de Pompadour, who before making her royal connection was a friend and admirer of Boucher, and had welcomed him to her soirées. If this claim was accepted, the painting would have had to be executed prior to 1744, for as the King's mistress

Mme de Pompadour (Wallace Collection)

from that year it is scarcely likely she would expose herself to the vulgar gaze; indeed it is unlikely that at any period in her life she sat for a painting in the nude, for Jeanne Poisson or Jeanne Le Normand d'Etiolles was a fastidious and not very sexually inclined young lady. Furthermore, neither the face nor the girlish figure bears the slightest resemblance to the Pompadour.

The most recent and certainly the most reliable and painstaking authority on Boucher, Jean Cailleux notes: 'on a vu successivement dans le personnage representé ici Madame de Pompadour et Victoire O'Morphi. Nous proposons de l'identifier avec la jeune Madame Boucher (Victoire O'Morphi ayant neuf ans quand cette peinture fut exécutée par Boucher) pour des raisons de ressemblance...' This assertion together with more recent evidence by the same author and based primarily on the question of resemblance is not quite correct and falls apart on at least one if not more issues. M. Cailleux first dates the painting 'L'Odalisque' as either 1743 or 1745. Accepting either date Jeanne Boucher, still very lovely and beautiful, was no longer in quite the category as then understood of 'la jeune Madame Boucher'. At the earlier date she was twenty-seven years old and at the later date twenty-nine. She was then the mother of three children, the oldest being about nine years old, and it is doubtful if Boucher used her as a model, particularly in a pose of this nature at this period, though there. is no doubt her face and head appeared on more lissome bodies many years later.

M. Cailleux makes an error when he states that Victoire O'Morphi was only nine years old in 1745. This mistake obviously arises from the fact that he confuses Victoire with her younger sister Louise who was about nine years old at that time. In point of fact, Victoire, who graduated from the Opéra-Comique, was fifteen or sixteen years old in 1745, and if the later date, which could be correct, was assigned to the painting she would be quite a mature, well-formed, young woman of the world.

Victoire was a seductive and alluring young woman when she became Boucher's *modèle en titre* and she undoubtedly shared his bed. Jeanne Boucher understood her artist husband and closed her eyes to his moral foibles. So well she might for about this time she was involved in a love affair of her own, and her paramour was no less a personage than the Swedish ambassador to the Court of France, Count de Tessin. The Count who was a patron of the arts gave many commissions to Boucher, and as a pretext for seeing and being with the lovely Jeanne commissioned Boucher to do the illustrations of the fairy tale of *Acajou*. He also commissioned the artist to do a series of illustrations for a poor and insipid novel he had written called *Faunillane, ou l'Infante Jaune*. Count Carl de Tessin's liaison with Jeanne Boucher lasted for a few years and was overlooked or connived at by Boucher who remained on very friendly terms with the ambassador and executed quite a number of commissions for him; this friendship accounts for the very fine collection of Boucher's paintings in the National Museum at Stockholm. During these few years Boucher enjoyed the warm companionship of his model Victoire O'Morphi.

'L'Odalisque' would appear to be the earliest painting in which Victoire was depicted. Some time later, perhaps because of the hostile criticism of Diderot and others, Boucher clothed his voluptuous nude, and transformed her into a Turkish woman, but he retained all the other details of the picture, much as Goya did in his celebrated 'Maja'.

It is not easy to identify all Boucher's models as there is a great similarity in them, and the better known features of the beautiful Jeanne would seem to be imposed on the bodies of much younger women, but it would seem Victoire was the actual model for the delightful 'Le Bain de Diane', 'La Toilette de Vénus' and 'The Sleeping Shepherdess'. Nolhac and Cailleux claim that Jeanne Boucher was the model for these and other paintings executed about the same time, mainly because of a slight resemblance in the features, but the lissome bodies are those of a very young woman not of a mature mother which Jeanne was. Undoubtedly she was remarkably pretty and beautiful up to middle age, but she could scarcely have passed for the youthful Venus and Diana whose slightly formed breasts and slender body could more accurately describe the nubile Victoire.

During the next few years, Boucher's fame as a society painter continued to grow, helped to a great extent by the rise to power of his patron and admirer Madame D'Etiolles who was responsible for his appointment to the post of *premier peintre du Roi*. Madame D'Etiolles' unique beauty and graciousness first attracted the attention of Louis XV about 1744, when he had a fleeting glance of the young lady who deliberately drove her carriage close to the hunting lodge where he was bound to see her. It was shortly after the death of the King's mistress, Madame de Châteauroux, that the calculating Toinette saw an opportunity of filling the vacant role, and possessing, as she certainly did, far more charm, ability and personality than any of the King's mistresses, she sought ways and means of being presented to him. The first real opportunity came on the occasion of a masked ball to celebrate the marriage of the Dauphin to the Infanta Marie-Thérèse-Raphaële. Every pretty woman in Paris crowded into Versailles in the hope of catching the King's eye. Toinette, looking very lovely, appeared at the ball as an exquisite and charming Diana 'matching, the statues in perfection of poised gesture and modelling, surpassing them all by the delicate carnation tints and the burnished gold of her curls'.

The King, struck by the elegant poise of the half-masked Toinette, asked her to raise her mask. Shy and coy for a moment, the glamorous Diana moved away, but suddenly turning to the King, she lifted the mask from her face. The King then recognised the lovely young woman whom he had seen so often in the grounds of Sénart where the royal hunt took place. Toinette instinctively knew the moves of the game, and turning quickly she ran from the ballroom. Some days later the King again met her at a ball — it was by arrangement — and when the dancing ended he asked where they could go in his coach. Being well brought up she told him he could take her to her mother's house. This the King did.

The machinations and intrigues of the court circle — now strongly divided between the austere and the voluptuaries who encouraged and flattered the King on one side, who prayed with and consoled the Queen and admired the goodness of the Dauphin, on the other side — were very real, and played a by no means unimportant role in the history of France and brought many new characters to the stage. Venus triumphed in the end however, and in due course Toinette found herself in the Court playing a part — for among other accomplishments she was a consummate actress — in the Comédie Italienne, privately arranged by the King. Shortly after this appearance she was installed first in an apartment in the Petit Cabinet and then in Versailles. A month or two later the Duc de Luynes, the elderly gentleman in waiting to the Queen, wrote: 'Madame is head over heels in love with the King, and this passion is mutual.'

Flushed by his victory over the English at Fontenoy, Louis XV returned in high spirits to Versailles, and had his new mistress presented at Court and accepted by all. Even the unfortunate Marie Leczinska, who henceforth played a very secondary role in the royal household, accepted her with pious resignation, saying that 'a bourgeoise become noble would prove less offensive than a noblewoman become prostitute'. She recognised however in the Marquise a woman of considerable charm and ability, and she was indeed personable, likeable and knew her place; she could quite easily be a friend and perhaps trusted confidante. At all events the long-suffering and cast-off Queen accepted the inevitable, and of all the women who had shared the King's bed the Pompadour was, so far as the Queen was concerned, the most acceptable of them all.

The Pompadour was not a compelling beauty — indeed there were more beautiful women in Paris — but she was vivacious, she had a charm of her own, and what few others possessed, she was highly intelligent, 'gifted with graces and talents'. She was a devotee of the arts, a superb and accomplished actress, and had the happy knack of satisfying every whim of an indolent King. With her natural and amiable charm she possessed him completely, imparting to him some of her own *joie de vivre*, thus helping to combat his natural ennui, satisfying not only his ever-urgent physical needs, but filling the mental vacuum which he suffered under a succession of mistresses of very mediocre ability and all too obvious quest for wealth and power.

The Pompadour had the good sense not only to ingratiate herself with the Queen, but to show to her on all possible occasions the deference and respect of a loyal and devoted subject. She presented herself like any courtier, spoke to the Queen respectfully, and offered whatever services should could render. It has been said that on occasion she upbraided the King for his neglect of his wife, and persuaded him to show at least some interest and gratitude, even to the extent of sending her choice blooms from the gardens and hothouses of Trianon. The Pompadour's interest and obvious understanding was not lost on the Queen, who, knowing her husband's appetites bore little or no grudge against a mistress who treated her with due regard, deference and politeness, and at times served perhaps as a weak link between herself and her husband.

The Pompadour had other qualities which eventually assured her a place in the annals of France which few other women in her position possessed. Unlike her predecessors she was for the most part singularly free from the petty intriguing which was so much part of court life, and she did not bring in her train a host of greedy and needy relatives, nor was she a place-seeker. True she did help some of her friends and supporters; her erstwhile protector Le Normand de Tournehem did receive an appointment, but her brother Abel Poisson, who was received at Court, and became a favourite with the King, was so embarrassed and confused with the intrigues, and the obsequious deference shown by the courtiers and the royal entourage that he retired to the family estate to live the quiet life of a country gentleman. Old François Poisson, the legal father of the Pompadour, who had been given a country estate, refused to accept a noble title, remarking that he was quite content to retain the family name since he had no pretensions to be anything but 'the father of the King's whore'.

Perhaps the Pompadour's greatest and only worthwhile contribution to France was her patronage of the arts and her real and genuine love for beautiful things. She was a woman of culture, an accomplished musician, a singer of some quality, an amateur artist, and a consummate actress. She enlivened a drearily amorous court by setting up a theatre in the *petits appartements*, and commissioned works from the foremost writers, including Voltaire, who though admiring her was not entirely *persona grata* with the Court. She retained the services of such artists as Boucher, La Tour, Nattier and Van Loo to decorate the walls and ceilings at Versailles, and she filled her own apartment on the second floor with their choicest works, particularly with the work of Boucher, whose sumptuous and highly suggestive paintings delighted the King.

The canvases commissioned and purchased by the Pompadour breathed all the beauty and elegance of the delicate rococo of the period. The sensuality and gallantry of the Court was exemplified, almost mirrored, in canvases whose flesh-tinted nudes in gay abandonment were as exciting as the models they represented.

When the Pompadour's passion for the theatre palled, her love of the beautiful and the artistic prompted her to plan new palaces and chateaux. For the next few years she lavished not only her undoubted talent but almost the entire coffers of the King on some of the loveliest buildings in Paris, buildings devised and laid out with exquisite charm and taste; there were gardens teeming with exotic plants and flowers, grounds graced with cascades, ravines and grottoes, menageries provided for rare animals, and delightful aviaries for strange birds. No less than eight such buildings were erected or altered by her at a cost of many million livres. The great architect Lassurance was her adviser, and Boucher and Van Loo executed superb ceilings and exquisitely painted panels.

As the Pompadour grew in stature and esteem her extravagance increased. 'No money is available for the fleet,' a contemporary complained, 'but the Favourite can spend great sums of money on trumpery buildings that one destroyed on the merest whim. Pensions and rewards were scattered broadcast, and enormous amounts of money were given for the smallest service. The expenses of the Court are increased without limit, the King's little journeys are ruinous, as much as 100,000 livres going in four days.' But the Pompadour, despite a growing unpopularity among the already heavily taxed people, held the King's affection firmly in her grasp, and could do simply as she wished.

Through the following years the Pompadour's power and influence extended even further, she dispensed her favours, sacked ministers as she pleased, and in the ever-growing field of royal patronage her word and wish was supreme; nothing was done nor any appointment made without her approval and consent. The King, who had almost ceased to rule, gratified her every whim with a nod and a smile, and fantastic sums of money poured out of the royal treasury. She spent one million livres on porcelain flowers for her house, and the King gave her as a present the village of Sèvres, and she had the famous porcelain works removed from Vincennes and established there, so that the manufacture could be carried out under her own supervision. With her coterie of brilliant artists, she was in a position to see that only the finest and most beautiful porcelain was produced.

The King, ever a restless and tiresome soul and slowly losing whatever popularity he had among his people, demanded more and more of his Favourite's time. When away from the hunting field, he continually required to be entertained, amused, distracted and continually petted like a spoiled boy. To these manifold and exacting tasks the Pompadour devoted her unerring skill, shrewdness and ability; thus she maintained her position as the first lady, despite the growing hatred of her among the hungry people of Paris, despite embittered and hostile courtiers who had been thrust aside and lived in real fear of her, despite the strong and far from silent condemnation of many clerics, particularly the Jesuits, who refused to hear her Confession and would not allow her to receive Holy Communion unless she openly and without question abandoned her role of mistress to the King, and returned to her neglected and cast-off husband. But the Pompadour feared neither the mob and their execrations, the courtiers and their intrigues, the instransigent Church and its excommunication, or the powerful Society of Jesus, and when Père de Sacy refused to absolve her in Confession, unless she showed herself truly penitent, and promised to abandon her sinful life she wrote:

'Mon père: — You show yourself a true Jesuit. How you must have enjoyed the embarrassment and need in which you have found me. I know how much it would gratify the Society of Jesus to force me to leave Court. This I will never do unless it should please the King to send me away. Understand that I am as powerful here as you, and that in spite of all the Jesuits in the world, here I will remain.'

And remain she did.

When the Pompadour had lost the first bloom and freshness of young womanhood, and was approaching her thirtieth birthday, there was still an imperious beauty about her; she was tall and stately with a slim figure, and she was finely featured, blessed with a captivating smile and a ready wit that held the King in thrall; he was as dependent upon her as a child upon its mother. She alone could chase away the heavy cloud of ennui enveloping him, and bring a smile to his face, dissipating his moroseness. When he grew weary, restless and bored, and complained of the tiresomeness of being King, she moved with him from palace to palace, from château to château. She had now accumulated no less than eight choice residences which she continuously decorated and re-decorated with the finest and most sensuous works of Boucher, some of which she felt would excite the at times jaded ardour of the King. She made all the arrangements for the continuous move from house to house, and was the admirable and capable hostess at the many petits châteaux where she and Louis lived in splendour.

The Pompadour's energy and activities were really remarkable, so much so that D'Argenson, Minister for Foreign Affairs, and perhaps one of the most reliable Court diarists, wrote. 'What prodigious labour! To rule the Kingdom, to govern the King, to deal with intrigues, petitions, places and pensions; to act, to hunt, to sup and ever be pleasant to the King... It is a miracle she can do all the things she must attend to.' In proof of this, if proof were needed, the Pompadour wrote to a good friend: 'You think that we do not travel any more; you delude yourself. We are always on the move, Choisy, La Muette, La Celle, the Hermitage... I pass half my life in carriages. I have not a moment, a single moment to myself... It is a terrible life, nevertheless I am happy, supremely happy, and that is all that matters.'

The Pompadour was indeed happy, life had given her almost everything, yet for some reason or other she was unable to bear a child to her royal lover. This was her most earnest wish and desire, for she felt that if she could bear children, they, more than anything else, would cement and strengthen the ties which bound her to the King. Wherein the failure lay it is difficult to say. She was not barren for she had conceived a daughter by her husband, and she would appear to have had a number of miscarriages, the last in 1749. When on that occasion she was told that she was very unlikely to have another child she was bitterly disappointed, and this disappointment, coupled with a feeling she might lose the King's affection, worried her somewhat. She knew she could keep the King amused, that she could provide the antidote to his continuous boredom by keeping him fully occupied, but to hold the fickle fancy of a sensualist was a different matter entirely. The Pompadour had some cause for anxiety. She was not entirely frigid, but she felt inadequate at times, and found it increasingly hard to accommodate herself to the almost continuous pathological ardour of the King.

To make good the deficiency in her nature, the Pompadour put herself on a special diet such as drinking hot chocolate, eating truffles and celery soup which were supposed to have a certain aphrodisiacal effect. She confessed to the Duchess de Brancas that she dearly loved the King, and wished at all times to please him, and appear attractive and desirable. 'I would gladly give my life to please him,' she confessed, 'but alas, he sometimes says I live up to my name — that I am as cold-blooded as a fish. Last week he spent many days on my sofa; he said it was the heat, but I know better. He will turn against me and take another mistress.' The Duchess advised the Pompadour against dieting and said: 'You will find other ways of holding your position. Be doubly agreeable to the King, and let time do the rest. The toils of habit will soon bind him to you.'

Shrewd beyond measure, the Pompadour realised in the early 1750s, that while in some respects she was well-nigh indispensable to the King, she could no longer match his wearisome appetite for love-making. To maintain her position, therefore, and at the same time satisfy the King, she advised him to use seductive grisettes when and as he pleased, carefully suggesting that by adopting this simple course, he would not involve or tie himself, and these nameless little love-birds would have but small claim on his largesse. There was a certain risk in this suggestion, but on the whole it seemed very slight. Ephemeral love affairs, the mere satisfaction of the moment would not unduly disturb her, and it was fairly clear that if her master found satisfaction in this way, he would be unlikely to turn his attention to the more sophisticated and beautiful court ladies who were waiting to supplant her; she knew there were many such aspirants.

How far the Pompadour should encourage the King to be satisfied with nameless grisettes must have given her some qualms. To perhaps encourage him in this direction and turn his mind to young voluptuaries, she commissioned Boucher to paint a number of erotic and titillating pictures with which to decorate her own and the King's apartments. Boucher, she knew, was as good a judge of a pretty face and a young, lissome body as anyone in Paris. The flesh-tinted bodies on his delightful canvases appeared so desirable, and yet so freshly innocent in their abandonment, that the jaded King expressed a desire to possess them. The Pompadour had no objection.

Louison

Off and on during a period of nearly five years, Victoire O'Morphi, the pretty brunette with the impish and provocative smile, flitted in and out of Boucher's atelier, and sat for some of his most delightful paintings. Though her features and body are clearly delineated in the artist's celebrated Coucher, she is also portrayed in some other paintings in which Maria Jeanne Boucher is the central figure, or at least her likeness, notably 'Retour de Chasse de Diana' and 'Le Leda', but Victoire found life outside the studio, even the exalted studio of Boucher, much more exciting and interesting. Her many love affairs left her with little time for the exacting life of a model, and when finally Claude Pierre Patu took her to be his mistress she more or less abandoned her role as Boucher's *modèle en titre* and occasional mistress.

However, one other member of the O'Morphi clan still continued to be a model and that was Brigitte, who was fully employed in the Academy. The Academy models were for the most part in a somewhat lowly category, many of them were simply prostitutes, or unsuccessful dancers from the Opéra-Comique, and they were at the beck and call of every young art student, and the less skilled artists who could not afford the exclusive use of a model of Victoire's class. How long Brigitte continued in this role and what she eventually did with her life is not known, for unlike the other members of the family she lacked beauty, and does not appear to have had a rich or well-to-do protector or lover like her sisters.

By the year 1750, Victoire was sufficiently well established and known as a model, an actress, a dancer of some ability and a young lady about town. She was much sought after by well-to-do young men, and had little time or inclination for the wealthy *roués* and voyeurs hanging about the Opéra-Comique and the Foire St. Laurent; she did, however, maintain a tenuous link with her former protector, St. Lubin, who was a man of influence and

37

substance, and could always prove helpful.

Though Victoire had many lovers she was at this time in love with Claude Patu, a successful young advocate in the Parlement of Paris, a wit and light-hearted writer. He was a charmer, a good companion and the first man to befriend Casanova when he visited Paris, and he introduced him to the right people. Unfortunately he was married and Victoire had to be content with the role of mistress. This liaison lasted for a few years in spite of Patu's gregarious nature and decided weakness for women including such well-known Parisians as the singer Marie Le Fel. On the occasion of one of his visits to the amorous singer who was the toast of Paris, he brought Casanova along with him and as Casanova had at the time little knowledge of Parisian life and ways he committed one of the many gaffes which he records with glee. Noting the beautiful children in her house he remarked on the fact that all three were very dissimilar in appearance. 'So well they might be,' she told him. The eldest boy is a son of the Duke of Ancenis, the second is the son of Count Egmont and the youngest is the son of Maisonrouge.' Casanova was silent for a moment and then remarked, 'I thought you were the mother of all three.' Marie Le Fel smiled, 'And so I am,' she said.

Patu's infatuation with women resulted in his early death, and Casanova recalls that the gay young man, 'introduced me to all the women of pleasure who enjoyed some reputation in Paris. He loved the fair sex as much as I did, but unfortunately for him he did not have as strong a constitution as mine and he paid for it with his life.'

He was scarcely thirty when he died, but shortly before this he introduced Victoire to Casanova, who records the occasion in his own inimitable way, and wrote: 'Taking it into his head to sup with a Flemish (?) actress by the name of Morphi he invited me to go with him. I felt no inclination for the girl, but I went in order to please my friend.' Victoire for reasons best known to herself, was living under the name of a former lover, St. Gratien, and had a house in the Rue des Deux Portes St. Sauveur, where her young sister Louise also lived, but was treated like a common drudge or servant and constrained to wait upon her sister.

After supper, 'Patu fancied a night devoted to a more agreeable occupation'. As it was rather late and Casanova did not wish to leave his friend, he asked for a couch on which he could sleep quietly for the night. While Patu enjoyed the comfort of Victoire's bedroom, Casanova was confronted by the precocious Louise whom he describes as 'a pretty, ragged, dirty little creature.' She was pretty, very pretty and only appeared dirty as she had waited on the party. She slept in a closet or garret such as might be occupied by a menial or serving girl, furnished only with a bed of four boards, and a mattress. There was a small skylight in the roof, and a few grubby prints on the rough walls.

The young girl offered her bed to Casanova for a Crown and he readily agreed but when he saw where she slept he turned on her.

'Do you call this a bed, my child?' he asked.

'I have no other,' she told him.

'Then I do not want it and you shall not have the Crown.'

Louise appeared disappointed, and Casanova asked her.

'Do you sleep with your clothes on?'

'Oh, no!'

'Well, then, go to bed as usual and you shall have the Crown. I want to see you.'

'Why?' she asked.

'I want to see you undressed.'

'Would you do anything to me?'

'Not the slightest thing,' he told her.

She thereupon undressed before the admiring Casanova who remarked that in her nakedness, 'the impression made by her dirty tatters disappeared and I only saw a perfect beauty, but I wanted to see her entirely. I tried to satisfy my wishes, but she resisted. However, a double Crown of six francs made her obedient, and finding that her only fault was a complete absence of cleanliness I began to wash her with my hands... I found the young Morphi disposed to let me do as I pleased except the one thing for which I did not care. She told me candidly she would not sleep with me because in her sister's estimation it was worth twenty-five louis.'

Unable to seduce the girl, Casanova was satisfied to fondle her, and he remarked that he found in her, 'a talent which had attained great perfection in spite of her precocity'.

Though the indefatigable amorist failed to seduce Louise who was somewhat older than he thought, 'and far from innocent', he was struck by her beauty, and told Patu that she was one of the most beautiful girls he had ever seen, and that they should visit her again, and see her in all her naked loveliness. A number of visits ensued, and Patu was compelled to agree with Casanova that, 'the chisel of Praxiteles had never carved anything more perfect... As white as a lily she possessed all the features which nature and the art of the painter can combine,' and 'the loveliness of her features were so heavenly that it carried to the soul an indefinable sentiment of ecstacy, a delightful calm'.

Victoire, though very much a woman of the world, light-hearted and pleasure-loving, was disturbed and not at all pleased by the interest Casanova displayed in Louise, for she knew he was a heartless seducer, and if his protestations of love prevailed the reward was not great. Furthermore, in pursuance of her own way of life she was finding the presence in the house of her young sister somewhat uncomfortable and a little embarrassing now that she had accepted Patu as more than a passing lover. To avoid embarrassment and at the same time give some protection to her young sister she appealed to her former protector, St. Lubin, to have Louise apprenticed to the dressmaker, Madame Fleuret, an ample and prosperous woman who dressed a number of fashionable ladies, and on the side procured pretty young girls for the entertainment of their husbands.

The drudgery, harshness and lack of freedom in Madame Fleuret's establishment did not appeal to Louise, nor did the unsavoury name of Madame Fleuret as a procuress find favour with the rest of the O'Morphi clan. Young as Louise was and despite her miserable bedroom, the cast-off clothing of her prosperous sisters, and almost Cinderella-like existence, she decided to return home for she was keenly aware of the extravagant, idle and fairly affluent life her sisters enjoyed. She felt, quite naturally, that in time some of the crumbs from the rich table would fall into her lap, and that she too might enjoy the exciting and seemingly rich life of the demi-monde.

Victoire still had no wish or desire to have Louise living with her, and she again appealed to her friend St. Lubin for help. This time Louise was confined to a convent, just as Victoire herself had been and was told she would remain there certainly until after her first Communion. The short confinement behind convent walls did not do Louise any harm, on the contrary it seemed to benefit her, and unlike her sisters she acquired a smattering of education, and some little poise and refinement which proved helpful in later years.

After six months, Louise left the convent and returned to a world of which she had some slight experience and not a little acquaintance. It was fairly clear and indeed obvious to her that there was no great virtue in modesty despite what the good nuns said in its favour; after all, her sisters were not shining examples of innocence and they had done very well for themselves. They may not have been wealthy but they had risen considerably above the lowly life of their childhood. Louise saw no reason why she should not do equally well if not better. Her mother, still working behind the innocent facade of an old clothes dealer, encouraged her for she too saw a promising future for the young girl who possessed a vibrant beauty and loveliness of her own, indeed she promised to be the fairest of the clutch.

Shortly after leaving the convent to which she had been committed, Louise was surprised to have a visit from Casanova whom she had completely ignored a year or so earlier. She was now, however, a more mature and provocative, young woman, and was living with her older sister Marguerite, at this time called Madame Melun, the name of her well-to-do protector, who was also a friend of Casanova's. Though Marguerite had assumed Melun's name she had not entirely dispensed with her former lover Meusiner. When Casanova saw Louise again he was once more struck by her beauty and describes her, 'as tall and well-built; her face has fine features, but is a little on the long side. Her hair is brown like that of her sisters, but she is not so pock-marked as they are. Louison works for her elder sister Madame Melun. When I saw her,' he continued, 'she was busy washing up, and her hands were dirty with cleaning her alleged brother-in-law's shoes.'

As Casanova watched Louise, or as he called her, Louison, he was so struck by her beauty that for a moment or two his mind and thoughts turned from his usual preoccupation, and he suggested she should accompany him to the studio of a well known painter to sit for him in the nude. Louise did not object, in fact both Marguerite and herself liked the idea. After all, her sister Victoire had been painted in the nude, and was now enjoying a comfortable life.

Casanova in his usual cavalier manner hustled Louison into his waiting carriage and drove to Boucher's atelier in his new house in the rue Richelieu, near the Palais Royal, and not far from the studio he had been allowed to use in the King's library under the Cabinet des Medailles. Boucher was delighted with his new model, 'whose beauty shone through the dirt and rags'. Since the departure of Victoire he had to be content with a series of little grisettes and had in fact no *modèle en titre*. However, when he saw Louise he immediately engaged her to sit for him. From this moment the youngest daughter of the former Irish cobbler of Rouen became Mlle. Louison O'Morphil, and filled a predestined role in the less savoury history of France.

Casanova in his inimitable and entertaining memoirs claims to be the one who brought the young and beautiful Louison to Boucher, but for reasons best known to himself says he brought her to the studio of a German painter who paid 6 louis to paint her in the nude. He writes: 'I paid 6 louis to have her painted naked by a German painter, who produced a living likeness. She was lying on her stomach resting her arms and her bosom on a pillow and holding her head as if she were lying on her back. The skilful artist had drawn her legs and thighs in such a way that the eye could not wish to see more.'

Casanova was not very accurate in his statements, and more often than not concealed the names of his friends in the anonymity of nationality, but there is no doubt that the so-called German artist was in fact Boucher. It is doubtful, however, if he completed a painting of Louison for Casanova; more likely he simply produced there and then the well-known sketch of the delightful model, a number of which exist, and from which eventually derived the better known painting.

Casanova was not the only one who claimed to have introduced Louison to Boucher, and we must remember that he was not unacquainted with the family. Where the claim to have made the original introduction lies is really of little consequence, but what we know is that towards the end of the year 1751 when Louison was just past her fifteenth year, Boucher saw her and was instantly struck by her unusual beauty. She was well developed for her years; she possessed a roguish smile, a straight forehead, an impish upturned nose, and there was an air of engaging innocence about her which Boucher liked, and he had no hesitation in engaging her as a model for she was a seductive creature, and enchantingly lovely.

At the outset he simply used his young model to fill in his great canvases with a retinue of nereids for the features of Jeanne Boucher continued to dominate as the central or principal figure in his paintings. Though almost seventeen years had passed since he first painted his wife the impression of her youthful charms never faded. Even now, at the approach of middle age, she was beautiful, but Boucher found the young, graceful body of his new model more suitable and lascivious for the great works he was presently painting with feverish activity. He found too that Louison was not without intelligence; she was quick and eager to learn, she had a sparkling and pleasant sense of humour, and under the skilled tutelage of Jeanne, who liked her, she began to play an important role in the artist's life and excite a certain amount of curiosity outside the studio. With the advent of Louise, Boucher had no further need for the grisette or dancing girls from the Opéra-Comique.

For the next few years, Louison added a fresh piquancy and charm to Boucher's pictures, and her quickly ripening body was extravagantly scattered here and there, in various poses, on innumerable canvases, which prompted the Abbé Le Blanc to exclaim: 'One wonders where Monsieur Boucher had found models of such exquisite beauty.' But there is no question of the plural, for the lovely and exciting bodies adorning some of his most sumptuous and provocative canvases around this time are those of a single model now affectionately called Louison, or le petite O'Morphi, by

Boucher and his friends who came to admire her. She was no longer the lowly daughter of an Irish cobbler and an ageing woman who still sold clothes in the Place du Palais Royal. Indeed it would seem she had cut herself more or less completely from the past, from her sisters and the shady flesh-pots surrounding them.

Many models had passed through Boucher's studio in the past, and he had treated them for the most part with little sentiment or feeling; they had come from the Opéra-Comique, from the alley-ways and back streets, and as a young man he had taken prostitutes from the Paris brothels. He painted them as he saw them, without sympathy, and when in the mood he used them, but few stayed long with him, particularly when the beautiful Jeanne so effectively took over her dual role as wife and model. Even Victoire O'Morphi was not fully employed by him, and certainly never occupied the place in his life and art that her young sister did.

From the outset, Louison fitted perfectly into Boucher's life; she was the ideal model, malleable, responsive, and ready to accept with almost childlike innocence any show of affection, love and regard bestowed upon her. In this way she suited every mood and fancy of the artist. In his paintings she appears as an innocent nymph, an impudent seducer, a charming goddess, a saint and a sinner, or a simple, guileless shepherdess. Even the Queen, Marie Leczinska, now deeply religious and wholly abandoned by her husband, saw her every day depicted in a painting of the Holy Family hanging in her private chapel. The Pompadour saw the provocative body, the smiling half-innocent face, the slightly upturned nose, scattered over the gallery of the Bellevue Palace which had just been decorated by Boucher and Van Loo. This gallery so beautifully and tastefully designed was filled almost entirely with Boucher's paintings, paintings that were linked together with garlands of carved wood patiently executed by the great master Verberckt. The King saw these paintings too and admired them as a voluptuary and lover of the flesh. What man could not be aroused by this lissome body with its provocative poses and flesh-tinted colours?

During the years 1751 and 1752, Boucher surpassed himself with his representations of Louison. In a year or two she had matured considerably, and at the age of seventeen was beautiful, with long, slender arms and legs, a perfectly fleshed body and well formed breasts. Altogether she was a captivating creature, and nobody appreciated this more than the artist whose work had now reached its most luminous and evocative stage.

During the few years Louison was engaged as his model Boucher produced some of his best known, though not necessarily finest, pictures. Among these were some delightful crayon sketches of Louison, including

Louise O'Murphi sur un Divan (*crayon sketch*)

perhaps his best known nude. 'Louise O'Morphil sur un Divan', which for grace and beauty far surpasses his 'Odalisque' which had shocked so many people, and was considered by Diderot, who was no mean critic, to be wholly unworthy of a great master, for he wrote: 'Didn't we see in the salon seven years ago, a woman completely naked, stretched out on pillows, one leg here, the other leg there, having a most voluptuous air.' He and others protested against this form of art, declaring that it was salacious, immoral and 'of the lowest rank of the Salon'. They were however condemning 'Odalisque', the representation of Victoire whose features, pose and insouciance had none of the grave, child-like, innocence of Louison, but then Victoire was very much the woman of the world.

The famous painting of Louison did not excite the same adverse criticism as 'Odalisque'. Indeed the fresh, young girl lying so nonchalantly, so delicately, appears thoughtful, and the easy restful pose lacks the self-conscious voluptuousness of many of Boucher's paintings. As well as this painting, Boucher did a series of sketches of Louison which showed slight variations in pose and these sketches served as master copies to be used later on innumerable canvases. He also did some small sketches of her face, hands and feet. Though the beauty of the young model is clearly revealed in all its loveliness in these sketches, it is in the larger pictures that she really comes to life, and is portrayed with all the innocence and abandonment of a child of nature who revels in the cool freedom of nakedness, like a nymph just emerged from its chrysalis.

Boucher submitted no paintings to the salon in 1751, but he painted as untiringly as ever. When he first met and was struck by the beauty of Lousion he was in fact at the height of his power, and had also reached a stage of accomplishment and certainty that he no longer required a model, and had more or less informed Reynolds that he had dispensed with them. He apparently changed his mind when Louison appeared, and with her coming he produced some of his best known paintings, including his 'Reunion des Génies des Arts', and 'Laons et Deios', or as it was later labelled, 'Evanouissement d'Amphitrite'. During this period too he was painting Venus pieces of exquisite quality in which 'the flesh tones upon the nude bodies of his goddesses were unsurpassed by mortal hands'.

In December 1751, Normand de Tournehem died, and the Pompadour appointed her brother, Abel Poisson de Vandières as Director General of buildings, houses, castles, parks, gardens, art and factories of the King. The young man brought to the office some of his sister's exquisite taste, talent, and foresight and did much for the advancement of art in France.

In the following year De Croy, who was the Director of the Academy of

France died, and the post and pension was secured for Boucher. Louison was now firmly established as his *modèle en titre*, and though he was busily engaged with the decoration of Fontainebleau, he found time to paint the superb canvas 'Two nymphs of Diana returning from the chase'. Fully occupied with many commitments, Boucher, who was always regarded as an excellent teacher, had at this time some of his most outstanding pupils. Perhaps the most brilliant of these was Fragonard whom Boucher encouraged to compete for the Prix de Rome which he won; he entered the Ecole des Elèves Protégés in 1753.

A great deal of the work of Boucher and his pupils, particularly about this time, bore a remarkable similarity, not only in style and texture, but in the actual employment and disposition of the figures. Many of Fragonard's earliest paintings have been attributed to his master who actually encouraged his students to copy him with slavish accuracy. It would seem therefore, certainly in the case of Fragonard, and the students Deshayes and Baudouin who later married one of Boucher's daughters, that they were permitted to use Louison as a model. This is fairly evident in Fragonard's 'Le Réveil de Vénus', 'Repos de Diana', and, 'Jupiter et Io', all of which were executed about this time, and have often been attributed to Boucher.

The years 1752 and 1753 were perhaps the busiest years of Boucher's active life. They were also years in which he fully employed his delightful young model. During these years, therefore, we hear little about Louison, and only see her depicted on one canvas after another. Besides painting Louison, Boucher made many sketches for the figures that were to adorn the ceilings at Fontainebleau. At the Salon in 1752, he exhibited among other works, his delightful Four Seasons and a superb Pastoral, and was hard at work on some of his largest and most luxuriant canvases.

Among these canvases perhaps the most famous and certainly best known in 'Le Lever de Soleil' which depicts Louison in a number of poses, and some of these have survived as delightful sketches. But it is in the painting itself we see the young model in her full radiant beauty. The critic, de Nodhlac writes: 'It is not Tethys or even Phebus who captivates our attention, however luminous they appear, it is the fresh retinue of Nereids. These models, their pretty bodies scattered around the God of light are of the same kind as the young O'Morphi. It is her likeness we see everywhere here, in the air, in the water, like a haunting delicious theme. On the right of the picture, shown low, lying on her side in the white foam she seems, in her glorious nakedness, the only flower of the day. On the left she is seen rising out of the clouds, and it is she who has just offered the lyre to Apollo.' These poses, richly bestrewn here and there, are but slight — very slight — variations of the immortal 'Louise O'Morphil sur un Divan'.

A companion piece, 'Le Coucher Soleil', painted in 1753, again depicts Louison in varying attitudes 'in her glorious nakedness'. De Nodhlac writes: 'She has her place also in the charming symbolism of "Le Coucher Soleil"'. This time the artist has reproduced one of the studies that he made of her when she shows the line of her back. But in this canvas, Téthys of a different age than O'Morphi and a different grace, attracts our attention more. Completely white she appears to hold the last rays of evening, while sitting on a seashell, with a sweet geature, she makes a sign of Phoebus. Her prettiness, her slim figure, her delicate air, recall the main features of Madame Pompadour herself; courtesy on the part of the painter no doubt!' Though the features are not unlike the Pompadour's or for that matter Jeanne Boucher, the slim young body with its small though well rounded breasts, could not belong to the now far from youthful Favourite, or even the lovely Jeanne, now a mature matron of thirty-seven. It is not improbable, however, that the Pompadour ever anxious — and more so about this time — of losing her power to attract, titillate and retain her hold on the King, had asked Boucher to paint her head and likeness but with the lissome and nubile body of his most evocative and desirable model.

Louison at this time was not unknown or entirely a stranger to Madame Pompadour who was a very frequent visitor to Boucher's atelier. He was not only her favourite painter, but had been her teacher; he taught her to draw and paint, and of all the portraits of her none equalled those by Boucher, who, though not a consummate portrait painter executed no less than five pictures of her, and it would seem that she figures as the Muse in the well know painting 'Muse Erato et Muse Clio'. Whether at the outset the Pompadour had any thought or design of taking Louison to the King it is difficult to say, but already sumptuous portrayals of her in various poses decorated some rooms at Versailles and Fontainebleau, and these did not pass unnoticed by the King.

Though Madame Pompadour chided herself because of her sexual cold-ness and the fact that she was not a very passionate woman, she did to some degree share the King's tastes and had a liking for the sensual, in-delicate and erotic, but she could no longer match the ardours of the voluptuous King, or satisfy him sexually. Despite this she maintained a stronger hold on his affections than even Madame de Mailly, who, when superseded by her sisters and other mistresses, still commanded the King's attention and lived platonically with him; it is said she occasionally went to bed with him followed by a quick dash to Confession. But the Pompadour had no wish to play such a secondary role, and fortunately her influence on the King was much stronger and more enduring than that of Madame de Mailly, even though his incessant love-making tired her and she had many miscarriages which may have made sexual relations difficult if not impossible. At any rate, about the beginning of the year 1752, the Pompadour moved into new quarters at Versailles and it was generally assumed she was no longer sleeping with the King, but her new apartments, like the old ones, had a secret staircase leading to the King's rooms.

Though Louis XV had reached middle-age and was as restless and as morose as in his younger days, his virility and sexual prowess had not diminished one whit. Deeply conscious of this the Pompadour decided to take a calculated risk to assuage the King's physical needs by providing him with suitable maidens who would be unlikely to supersede her, or be ambitious or scheming enough to aspire to the position of *maîtresse en titre*. Instinctively she knew the King was attached to her; that her sparkling wit, her gay vivacity, *joie de vivre*, and personal charm suited him admirably, and was an antidote to his boredom. A bed companion for Louis need not be a woman of rank or great beauty, and thinking along this line the Pompadour nurtured the idea that a series of pretty, young girls could be engaged to satisfy the King without adding to his responsibilities, or putting an undue strain on the royal purse already heavily committed.

The task of finding satisfactory *jolies filles* for Louis was entrusted by Dominique-Guillaume Lebel, Concierge de Versailles, the King's confidant and valet de chambre and an obsequious lackey of the Pompadour. Lebel was a rather shady character, but he served his master well and indeed any of the courtiers who needed his help. For more than twenty years, Lebel had kept his eyes open for pretty girls, not only for the King's delectation but for courtiers unable to search openly for suitable grisettes for a night's entertainment. Further, he was a scandal-monger and a noted raconteur of risqué stories. Lebel's first assignment or request for a bed-companion was shortly after the King's marriage when he had grown tired of the Queen's coldness, and the odd piousity which enabled her to rule that her husband could not have her on the feast days of major saints; in time these major saints became so numerous that they were in a fair way to making a celibate of him as they filled all days of the calendar. Outraged by this religious interdict, the King flew into a rage and demanded that Lebel find a woman for him, and this he did in the person of a pretty little housemaid, who later gave birth to Dorigny 'le Dauphin', who in time became a noted art dealer.

The Pompadour was not unduly perturbed by the procession of dull, little grisettes obtained by Lebel. She made it her business to see that they were empty-headed young girls, not particularly attractive, who after a week or two could be sent away with a piece of jewellery and a bag of money as a reward. She relied entirely on Lebel to use his discretion in his choice of girls, and at the same time ensure the complete anonymity of the girls' lover, which of course he did. There was just the danger, however, that Louis might weary of this succession of strange girls: this was a real problem, difficult to provide or guard against and therefore it had to be faced. Momentarily the Pompadour intervened, and her choice of somebody likely to fill the part fell on Boucher's young model Louison. She had seen the young girl in the artist's atelier, and was well acquainted with her appearance in Boucher's sumptuous paintings; the King too may have expressed a wish to meet the young model. Lebel also knew Louison, possibly through his friend Casanova, who though not of the court circle was much the man about town, and very probably showed Lebel the picture he had obtained of the young model, and from which numerous engravings had been made. Indeed, the engraving of 'La Petite O'Morphi sur un Divan' was thought a naughty picture, and was hidden in not a few cabinets to be brought out on suitably convivial occasions and passed from hand to hand.

Thus, sometime in the year 1753, at the age of seventeen, Boucher's seductive model was introduced to Louis XV.

The King's Mistress

Neatly dressed in a new silken gown with a cloak to match, Louison O'Morphi was taken by carriage to a private apartment in the north wing of the Royal Palace of Versailles overlooking the well-trimmed lawns, and not very far from the *Petits Appartements*. Though it was in the dark of night the coachman made a long and circuitous journey to his destination. The excited young girl, escorted by Lebel, had no real inkling as to the purpose of her nocturnal journey. Lebel, after a number of visits to Boucher's atelier, had already won the confidence of Louison, chatted amiably and told her he was taking her to a party or supper which was to be given by a distinguished Polish nobleman. This nobleman, he informed her, was a relative of the Queen, and having seen her so delicately depicted by Boucher had expressed a wish to meet and entertain her; she should therefore be nice to him. Louison, despite her age, was not an innocent young woman unused to the ways of the world, and particularly strange men who asked to see her. She had grown up in a household where her sisters entertained many men; moreover Boucher had made love to her. When, therefore, Lebel asked her to accompany him, he hinted that it would be worth her while to meet this wealthy man, and she fully understood what he meant.

The redoubtable Casanova claims to have played a major role in bringing the young model to the King and in effecting the introduction. In his account of the initial meeting he states that 'a proposition was made to Louison's older sister Marguerite, very much a woman of the world of love, who there-upon tastefully dressed her young sister, and primed her in her duties'. He also states that Marguerite accompanied Louison in the coach, and on reaching the private apartment at Versailles she handed her over to Lebel who was waiting in the courtyard. He then escorted her to a small, tastefully, furnished room, where she was told to wait the arrival of the Polish gentleman who wished to meet her, in the meantime she was to enjoy herself with a box of sweetmeats. Casanova's details are not correct, and his role in the whole affair was very slight, at most he was a friend of Lebel and knew Louison, whom he failed to seduce in her less affluent days.

After a short wait the King entered the room where Louison sat sucking a sweet. He was still a rather handsome man though inclined to a slight middle-aged corpulency. He smiled affably, and to put Louison at her ease he engaged her in small, trivial talk. He spoke about her work as a model, expressed admiration for her master, and told her he had seen many paintings portraying her. He produced from his pocket a small engraving of the famous 'La petite O'Morphil sur un divan' and showed it to her; it was an overt suggestion to expose herself. More than probably he compared the engraving with the young woman standing before him. The features might have changed little but the lissome and enticing body would have matured somewhat as a year or two had elapsed since Boucher had executed his painting; she would be more desirable now and had acquired a more subtle understanding of the finer points of love-making not only from her experienced sisters and the advice of her mother but from more experienced lovers such as Boucher.

While the King engaged her in small talk and relished what was to come, Louison studied his features closely for a while, then it suddenly dawned on her that the stranger was not a Polish gentleman at all but actually the King of France — Louis the well-beloved. With all the naturalness of an uninhibited girl she laughed out loud. Her laughter may have surprised the King used to silent, completely submissive, creatures who surrendered their bodies to him with no display of pleasure. Louison on the other hand was a seductive little creature and her uninhibited laughter fascinated him. Whether this warm and friendly attitude resulted from careful priming by Lebel or the more experienced Marguerite it is not easy to say, but later events tend to suggest that all her actions were perfectly natural and stemmed from the warm and passionate nature with which she was endowed.

The King was really pleased with the blue-eyed girl who was enchantingly lovely, more lovely than Boucher had depicted her or Lebel described her, and at the same time she was friendly, light-hearted, with a warm smile and, even in the King's presence, perfectly at ease. Indeed he possibly found her as Casanova did when he recalled that 'the loveliness of her features were so heavenly that it carried to the soul an indefinable sentiment of ecstasy'.

Resisting for as long as he could the sublimation of his passion, Louis took the young girl on his knee and began to fondle her. She did not resist his overtures or appear unwilling to enjoy his love-making but evinced as Casanova once noted a talent which had attained great perfection in spite of her precocity. Occasionally, however, she burst into ripples of laughter as though very amused. This was a little upsetting and the King looked at her with puzzlement; none of the grisettes or nigh innocent girls provided for his delectation in the past would have dared to laugh or even smile in his presence. He looked at Louison and, frowning, asked her if she knew who he was. She nodded her head and smiled in her friendly way.

'Who am I?' he asked again.

'You are as like a six-franc piece as two drops of water,' she told him.

It was the King's turn to laugh, and there and then he dropped his assumed anonymity. Clearly he was no longer dealing with a dumb-witted grisette, and he appreciated the fact. Here, making love to him, was a pert, quick-witted, girl who, given a little time, would grow in poise and self-assurance and might even rival the Pompadour. At the moment, though his mistress could not satisfy him physically nor assuage his sensual appetite, the King had no thought of anyone superseding or supplanting the Pompadour. Life without her would be very empty and very dull. She alone could provide a palliative for his constant ennui; she alone could sparkle in the boring court circle, and provide the companionship he so badly needed. Even if she lacked these qualities she could not be quite so easily cast aside. But as the King fondled the little beauty on his knee he decided that she would be a wonderful plaything, a *maîtresse en titre* perhaps to make up for what the Pompadour lacked; suitable arrangements could undoubtedly be made which would be acceptable to all concerned. Enamoured as he was, the King cast discretion to the wind, and asked Louison if she would like to stay in the palace or in an apartment he would set up for her, and be his friend; he assured her he would look after her and treat her well.

What Louison's reactions were to the King's invitation or suggestion we do not know, but she obviously realised she had everything to gain and nothing to lose by accepting him, and doing what she could to please and satisfy him. Even if the King decided later on to cast her aside, she could at least sustain his interest for a while. No doubt it pleased her to think that in accepting the proposal of so august a person as the King she was doing better, much better, than her sisters with all their sophisticated ways. Who after all were their men and masters beside the King of France? She knew them all. Meusenier the feeble, dandified, gambler and friend of Casanova, the colourless Melun, old enough to be her grandfather, the third-rate actor Corbier, the lawyer Patu, and poor President St. Lubin, a kind man, who had been cuckold by his nephew, a *soi-disant* Polish count, Patocky, and of course the self-assured Casanova who tried to seduce her. There was a host of others passing through the *ménage* presided over by her ambitious mother, who despite her bulk and age was not averse to accepting herself the blandishments of the aged *roués* who found the younger members of the family too much for them. The King on the other hand, was a handsome man, and from her brief experience he was kind and generous and gentle with her.

The following day the King consulted with Lebel, his pander-in-chief, and expressed himself satisfied with the young woman with whom he had spent the night. He also expressed a wish that she should be installed in the apartment which was now known by the sobriquet of *Le Trébuchet* — the bird snare — and where for many years, so it was claimed, a number of young girls without birth or breeding, but with certain other charms had been installed as members of a kind of miniature brothel or harem. Lebel was instructed by the King to see that the apartments were re-decorated and refurbished, and all traces of the former inhabitants removed. When this was done, he made the necessary arrangements for the comfort of the new arrival. Besides providing for Louison's comfort Lebel was instructed to make a satisfactory settlement with her mother, and this required considerable tact on Lebel's part, for he had to assure all and sundry that the young girl was not being ill-used, nor was she simply the plaything of the King to be cast aside when finished with.

Lebel first interviewed the shrewd and astute Margaret Murphy. She naturally professed a great sense of loneliness at the loss of her youngest daughter, attempted tears, and then endeavoured to convince Lebel of her dependence on her youngest daughter now that she was growing old and unable to work for herself. In the end, however, she was willing to accept a gift of 1,000 écus. Casanova claims that this sum of money was paid to Louison's older sister Marguerite in whose house Louison lived, and that it was Marguerite who dressed the young girl, and prepared her for her first visit to the King. Some of this claim may be correct for it is doubtful if the old clothes dealer would have been able to dress up her daughter and prepare her for entry to a noble household, but it is very unlikely that the old woman, who knew the value of money, would let herself be left out in the final settlement.

With all the more intimate details carefully arranged to everyone's satisfaction, Louison was installed in comfortable apartments, but she was very closely guarded against prying eyes and malicious tongues. The unctuous chief of the secret police let it be known publicly that the young girl had simply disappeared from her sister's house in the rue Saint Sauveur and had not been seen for some weeks. He also let it be known that the girl's mother was in receipt of a small pension, given by a gracious King to the widow of a gallant Irishman of good birth who had served in the French army. To lend veracity and verisimilitude to the story a police report was widely circulated to the effect that the pretty, little model, who was fairly well known, had fallen into the hands of a *souteneur* who was exploiting her. The story of the disappearance, somewhat embellished, did not excite much comment and after the initial hue and cry was completely forgotten.

In the meantime Louison had settled down 'comfortably in her new apartments. She pleased the King, and as she played her part to his entire satisfaction, she acquired a degree of permanence and security. Louis continued to be kind and gentle, and lavished trinkets and a certain amount of affection upon her. Louison made no great demands on his generosity, for she was quite happy in her own easy, light-hearted way, and made no effort whatsoever to assume a role of importance as *Maîtresse en titre*, or seek the confidences of her master.

In March 1753, she was installed in a small, comfortable house at Versailles, though according to the police inspector Meunser (not to be confused with Marguerite's lover) only a few of the King's more intimate friends knew of the actual existence of the house, which was number 17 rue d'Anjou at the corner of the rue de Hansard. A few years earlier this unpretentious house had been in the possession of a court official, and was very possibly purchased for Louison. It was of modest proportions 'where the wife of a government official might live with several young people without arousing the curiosity of the public'. The house was a three-storey building with four rooms on each floor, a courtyard with stables, and a garden well planted with trees. Louison was quite content to settle down in her new home, and having no ambitions whatsoever, she was happy in simply playing her part as a beguiling and entertaining mistress. It was not an onerous task and was pleasurable enough. If she found it a little tiresome and demanding at times she was well recompensed for the trouble. She had a nice house now and was waited upon by a maid, a housekeeper, and a lackey; she had a good cook too, for it would appear that Louis was wont to eat with her, and he insisted that Louison should live the life of a lady of ease, especially one favoured by the King.

By and large, Louison enjoyed and savoured her life of relative affluence and her relations with the King were warm, friendly and intimate. Each morning she went driving in a carriage brought especially from the Royal livery. On Sunday morning, like other well-to-do Parisians, she attended Mass, with at least outward devotion, in the Church of St. Louis. She dressed rather simply and, though extremely pretty and vivacious, attracted very little attention to herself or the role she played in the King's life. She was not presented at Court for the Pompadour was adamant on this, nor was she openly introduced to Court officials as was more or less usual in the case of those in royal favour. The Duc d'Ayen, the King's favourite crony, gossiper and retailer of *risqué* and really bawdy stories, was however permitted to meet her as a great favour and he was struck not only by her beauty and vivacity but her apparent innocence and guilelessness; she seemed entirely without ambition and quite happy and content with the role she played. More important still she satisfied the King and contained his ardour.

To read through the mass of intimate diaries, the pile of private dossiers and the revealing and scandalous memoirs of a number of strange and odd people who were deep in the centre or on the periphery of the court circle, reveals such a divergency of opinion, such dubious and doubtful statements, such final judgments and conclusions, that it is difficult, if not impossible to separate fact from fiction. For instance Casanova in his inimitable *Storia della mia vita* claims all the responsibility for introducing Louison to the royal seraglio and discovering and enjoying her hidden charms 'though leaving her a virgin'. He makes other unsubstantiated claims but perhaps the claim or statement of a number of gossiping scribblers that the house in the rue d'Anjou where Louison was installed also housed a number of other nubile girls for the King's pleasure and later became known as the notorious Parc aux Cerfs which has been described by d'Angerville and others as Louis' little harem. In point of fact, Louison's house in the rue d'Anjou must not be confused with the Parc aux Cerfs which was situated in the rue St. Médéric, and was formerly part of a deer park between rue St. Satory, rue des Rossignols and rue St. Médéric. The Parc aux Cerfs was a relatively new house, and was built about 1712 by Joseph Desnoues, and passed through several hands before being purchased for the King through a certain Francois Villet on the 25th November 1755.

It would seem therefore, certainly during the years 1753 and 1754, that even the ardent Louis was quite content with his new young mistress and did not require a number of grisettes to satisfy him. He was a frequent visitor to Louison and spent many hours each week in her apartments and had reached a stage when he no longer attempted to conceal his actions. In the course of time the frequency and duration of his visits appear to underlie a growing regard and affection for her, and Louison's name began to crop up more frequently in court circles until she became a subject of the kind of court intrigue which could, and did eventually, contribute to her downfall, intrigues which the Pompadour as a shrewd and more purposeful woman was capable of dealing with.

In the meantime, Louison continued to hold the King's favour and, it would seem, his affection. She made no demands on his generosity, nor sought any favours; she remained aloof from the court and the intriguing courtiers who would dearly like to gain access to her. The King found her amusing, and for a young woman without background it was no small accomplishment to be able to relieve his boredom. Also, she was by all accounts fond of the King, and she was passionate, vigorous and healthy. Her simplicity is clearly indicated by the fact that she was not ambitious, did not look too much to the future, nor did she think of the position of power within her grasp if she played her cards well; there was little to stop her achieving the standing of a Pompadour, if she wished.

Louison, pretty and engaging as she was, lacked most of the attributes and down-to-earth requirements that might have helped her to attain a position of *l'Eminence grisé* and influence over the King like others before and after her. Despite her experience and background there was a certain naivety about her, a childlike innocence. She was, of course, uneducated, and could barely read or write, and at times she spoke the common *argot* of the back streets. Indeed her idle chatter, her ungrammatical sentences, even her accent was being assimilated and unconsciously picked up by the King. It is recorded that the Pompadour's personal maid, Madame du Hausset, remarked to her mistress on one occasion that 'the King does pick up the most extraordinary expressions, for instance *"il y a gros"*,' and she added: 'He picks them up from those young ladies.'

The Pompadour thought this highly amusing, smiled and nodded her head. *'Il y a gros,'* she repeated.

The Marquis d'Argenson, who had been Minister for Foreign Affairs, was a shrewd observer of the French Court, and though now out of favour, still managed to retain a number of friends to keep him informed of what was happening in Court. Naturally he speculated with interest and not a little hope, that the intimate relationship between Louison and the King would result in the downfall of the Pompadour who had grown increasingly unpopular not only in court circles, but among the populace at large. Toward the end of April 1753 d'Argenson wrote in his diary: 'The King's love for the little Morfi continues and increases, but is still carried on with much mystery and secrecy.' This was true, for the King was being extremely careful and had no wish to offend the Pompadour, or ostentatiously set up a rival and thus create factions for there were already signs of dissident groups, or at least a clique prepared to do all it could to oust the Pompadour.

The King wanted harmony at all costs and desired no interference with his private pleasures which were entirely personal and were not to be spoken about or discussed. For some reason or other the gossiping crony and story-teller, the Duc d'Ayen, the King's boon companion for many years and his partner in a number of escapades in the past had been permitted to meet Louison and knew something about what was happening behind the scenes. In taking d'Ayen into his confidence the King was foolish and it would seem that d'Ayen in his cups boasted of his knowledge of the King's new mistress, and told his audience what a ravishing creature she was and most acceptable to the King. Though d'Ayen boasted of his knowledge, since it possibly helped his ego, he was not one to bear any ill-will or grudge against the Pompadour, on the contrary he was loyal and devoted to the Marquise, but what he said about Louison and the King's now frequent visits to her created quite a stir and a few nodding heads.

Some few months after the earlier entry in his diary d'Argenson wrote: 'The King is more and more in love with the little Morfi. She amuses him and that is very important indeed.' Clearly Louison was making progress and the King was becoming increasingly enamoured and finding her more and more satisfying. She was undoubtedly assuming a role the Pompadour never for a moment anticipated or thought possible. Heretofore the innumerable grisettes served one purpose only, and the Pompadour from the beginning regarded Louison as probably a little more acceptable than the more common grisettes but most unlikely to win the King's affection, or even regard, and simply dismissed her as one of her master's expendable playthings.

As the months went by, however, Louison grew prettier, more mature, and gained a good measure of the King's affection. Emboldened and perhaps to show his pleasure and recognition he began to appear with her in semi-public, and ceased to conceal her from at least his closest friends who were thus able to see that she was no ignorant grisette brought to the King to satisfy his passion for a night or two, but an attractive young lady with an exuberant charm of her own. On the occasion of Louison's eighteenth birthday the King gave a tea-party in her honour, and had her conveyed by coach to Crecy, one of the Pompadour's specially designed small and more intimate palaces and where she was actually in residence at the time.

This overt — almost challenging — action caused a slight ruffling and not a little stir in the inner Court circles. There were some who thought the King was going a little too far, in fact behaving in a very foolish and malicious manner by openly showing his interest in and appreciation of his young mistress. The Pompadour was annoyed, as well she might be, and suggested that the King's new mistress should be confined to her own apartments and he should only entertain and visit her there. Louis on the other hand preferred Louison to the grisettes; he actually liked her and found her entertaining and physically satisfying. He therefore saw no reason, despite protests and the admonitory words of his confessor, why Louison should not be conveyed to whatever residence had been chosen for his sojourn. After all the continuous movement from palace to palace was not entirely of his choosing but was dictated by the Pompadour and court etiquette. He was agreeable to conform, do his duty properly, and it was not asking too much to bring his little plaything with him. Lebel and d'Ayen agreed since they never opposed the King, and at the same time they felt that the Pompadour's power was waning.

Durini, another well-known gossiper and diarist, reported Louison's presence at Crecy in the autumn of 1753 and noted in his diary: 'There have been such scenes that everyone thought that the Favourite would have taken the part of retiring of her own accord without waiting to be thrown out.' Obviously the King was openly flaunting his new mistress and doing little if anything to conceal his infatuation, even though his conduct was giving rise to the scenes described by Durini, and resulted in much speculation on the part of those close to the King and comprising the inner Court circle.

The Pompadour, though very annoyed felt sufficiently sure of herself and the place she occupied in the King's affection, played her cards so astutely that she neither thought of retirement nor feared banishment; at worst she felt assured the King would acknowledge her as the *dame du palais* while the more lowly position of *maîtresse en titre* would be occupied by Louison.

Early in 1754 the King and his Court moved to Fontainebleau and Louison accompanied him. Durini noted this and jotted down in his diary: 'The new Irish star was to go to Fontainebleau where she has an apartment prepared for her. She receives diamonds, presents and magnificent dresses. Her emergence at full daylight was awaited by the nobles and the courtiers.' Among those who looked forward with eagerness to the rise of a new star, and was busily intriguing to this end, was the Marechale d'Estrées. Reports and rumours were rife that Louison was actually superseding the Pompadour and was also gaining the King's confidence. Despite the rumours the Pompadour still exerted a strong influence on Louis, and though she had many enemies she was well supported by a number of friendly courtiers close to the King, and these included François Quesnay the King's physician who when approached to side against the Pompadour, remarked tartly: 'I have been attached to Madame de Pompadour in prosperity, and I shall remain so in her disgrace.'

With the fluctuations and uneasy stirrings in Court the Pompadour came to terms with the King, and as a result was able to ensure that his affection was not too openly displayed, and to avoid too much scandal and gossip Louison continued to occupy her own apartments and did not appear openly at Fontainebleau.

There may, of course, have been another reason for Louison's confinement to her apartments other than the influence exerted by the Pompadour for it was widely rumoured now that she 'showed symptoms of pregnancy'. A month or two later the persistent rumour turned out to be true, and the King gave instructions that proper arrangements should be made for the accouchement.

Accepting his new responsibility for the unborn child, Louis consulted with the Pompadour. Madame du Hausset wrote: 'Madame called me one day into her closet where the King was walking up and down in a very serious mood. "You must," she told me, "pass some time in a house in the avenue St. Cloud, whither I shall send you. You will find there a young lady whom we wish you to attend with care." While Madame spoke to me the King paced the room in silence. Madame continued, "You will be the mistress of the house and preside at the accouchement. Your presence is necessary in order that everything may pass off secretly, and according to the King's wish. You will be present at the Baptism, and name the father and the mother." The King stopped his pacing, and began to laugh, and then he said lightly and knowingly: "The father is a very honest man beloved by everybody, and adored by those who know him." He turned to Madame, and taking her hand in his he pressed it to his lips. Turning again to me, serious now, he said: "Guimond will call upon you every day to assist you with advice, and at the critical moment you will send for him. You will say you expect the sponsors, and a moment later you will pretend to have received a letter saying they cannot come. You will, of course, affect to be most embarrassed."'

Whilst Louis appeared willing to accept paternity the Pompadour prevailed upon him to cloak the event in the upmost secrecy, and Madame du Hausset as the faithful and close servant of the Pompadour was sworn to secrecy. She was instructed that under no circumstances was Louison to be permitted to see or handle the child when it was born. She was also warned by both the King and Madame de Pompadour that 'you must not leave the young lady until she is safely delivered, and even then you must remain with her until she is restored in health'.

Madame du Hausset, so long now the Pompadour's personal maid, helpmate and confidante, had been assigned a new and somewhat delicate task. This was the first time that she had been asked to attend the accouchement of any of the King's young paramours for few of his natural children were ever acknowledged, and usually the young mother, while liberally paid for her service, received little or no attention, and no responsibility was attached to the King. Madame du Hausset's only experience of an accouchement was at the childbed of her mistress and these painful occasions were marked by miscarriages and the attendant severe haemorrhages.

When the time arrived for the birth of Louison's child Madame du Hausset carried out her instructions to the letter and then thoughtfully placed it all on record. She wrote: 'I went that evening to the avenue de Saint Cloud where I found a nurse, a wet nurse, two old men servants and a girl who was something between a servant and a waiting woman.' This would seem to have been the first occasion that Madame du Hausset set eyes on Louison and though she could not be unaware of her existence it is doubtful if she knew what she looked like or had ever met or spoken to her before. Face to face with Louison who was very near her time, Madame du Hausset noted: 'The young lady was extremely pretty and dressed very elegantly, but not too remarkable. I supped with her and the mother abbess who was called Mother Bertrand. I presented the aigrette which Madame de Pompadour gave me shortly before supper, which had greatly delighted the lovely, young lady, and she was in high spirits.'

It is hard to know whether the Pompadour's gift was something in the nature of a pay-off or a genuine mark of appreciation, for Louison had made the King happy and did not obtrude herself unduly. Though the King had shown a certain amount of affection and solicitude for Louison, the Pompadour felt sufficiently confident that no matter how much Louison pleased her master there seemed little likelihood that she would or could supersede her, even though it was rumoured that certain courtiers such as the younger d'Argenson, the Comtesse d'Estrades and the Maréchale d'Estrées were intriguing against her and endeavouring to gain access to Louison. The Pompadour, however, took a firm stand and as d'Argenson noted: 'She dominates the King as strong personalities dominate weak ones.' By her firm stand it had been possible to keep the King's young mistress in her place, and she had seen to it that Louison had not been presented to the Court, and on the few occasions that the King brought her with him on his change of abode, she only appeared before a few, a very few intimate friends. At this precise moment, in child-bed, it may have occurred to the Pompadour that after the birth of the baby, the King may conceivably tire of Louison, particularly if during the confinement and period of recuperation, he was constrained to take his pleasures elsewhere and find a suitable grisette. It was a shameful expedient, but as the Pompadour said to Madame du Hausset, 'All these little, uneducated girls will never take him from me.'

Louison was slow in bringing her baby into the world and the waiting period seemed interminable for the young expectant mother, but she had every care and comfort lavished on her. Small presents reached her almost daily from both the King and the Pompadour. 'On the sixth day,' Madame du Hausset wrote, 'she was brought to bed and according to my instructions she was told that the child was a girl, though in reality it was a boy. She was soon to be told that it was dead in order that no trace of its existence might remain for a certain time. It was eventually to be returned to its mother.'

All the arrangements worked out satisfactorily but a mystery still remains. Meunser, the police chief reported that 'the first result of the King's passion was a miscarriage, and the King is said to be inconsolable'. On the other hand Walpole writing to Richard Bentley on May 18th, 1754, notes that 'Mme Murphy is delivered of a prince and is lodged openly at Versailles'. Whatever the truth of the matter it would seem that the King had a considerable regard for Louison, and apparently desired a child who would combine the beauty and liveliness of his young mistress with his own good looks and virility. We must assume, however, that Meunser's report was correct for Louison was one of the very few bedmates of the King whose children were acknowledged and recognised by him.

With her abundant and natural good health, Louison quickly recovered from the effects of childbed, and was soon receiving the King with indecent regularity in her pretty apartment. She had reached an exciting maturity, was more beautiful and desirable than ever, and despite the loss of her child was just as gay and light-hearted as on the first day she was brought to the King. Her gaiety was not the sophisticated gaiety of the Pompadour, but the natural exuberance of a carefree young girl, and with her warm and ardent nature she not only amused the King but gave him satisfaction. Had she at this moment when the King was glad and delighted to have her again even a fraction of Madame's *éclat*, her cultured attributes, her fine accomplishments, her poise and manner the strong and dominant nature which characterised the Pompadour and gave her power not only over the King but most of the courtiers, she might have superseded the first lady, or at least shared her place with the King. Louison, however, was easy-going, a young, light-headed woman who was quite content to be loved by the King, giving her body freely for the luxury of living like a lady, and gladly accepting his presents as the mark of his appreciation.

Louison was at no time particularly ambitious and really wanted no more than the certain security of a comfortable home, servants to wait upon her and the King's affection and regard. In present circumstances she was infinitely better off than her sisters, and being young and light-hearted as well as thoughtless the future was too dim and distant to worry about; besides the King had assured her that she would be looked after and she had nothing to fear. She never questioned his assurance for she found him at all times generous and he had always treated her well. Of political affairs, the intrigues of the Court, the idle and malicious gossip and the great world beyond her apartment she knew and cared nothing. The persuasive voice of Louis, the raillery and flattery, sufficed, and she carried out her accustomed but by no means onerous duties to her own and the King's entire satisfaction.

Oddly enough the Pompadour accepted Louison and apparently at this stage had little or no fear of being supplanted by the King's Irish mistress. On the contrary she accepted the fact that Louison could satisfy a need of the King's which she was not particularly enamoured of. This acceptance is vouched for in the course of a letter from Walpole to Bentley already quoted in which he says: 'I don't believe that Mademoiselle Murphy and Madame de Pompadour will mix the least grain of ratsbane in one another's tea.'

Towards the end of the summer of 1755, Louison was again confined, and the discreet Madame du Hausset performed the self-same task as she did a year before. There were presents from the King, and the Pompadour sent gifts and her good wishes. The child born of this second confinement was a girl, but the young mother was not permitted to hold or even see the child. In accordance with the instructions given to Madame du Hausset the baby was whisked away to a wet nurse within minutes of its birth, and brought to the convent of the Presentation in the rue des Postes.

To digress for a moment from Louison, who, following her confinement and the disappearance of her infant daughter, returned once more to her former role, the infant when placed in the convent had an annuity of 8,000 livres provided by her father the King. The good nuns to whom the child was entrusted were unaware of her paternity, but were told the father was a high-ranking Frenchman who expressed a wish and gave instructions that his daughter should be brought up and educated in a manner befitting a noble woman, and ample provision, besides the annuity, would be available for this purpose. Louison's forgotten daughter was christened Agathe-Louise Saint-Antoine de Saint-André, thus combining the names of both of the King's mistresses.

A number of years were to elapse before the daughter of Louise O'Morphi was to take her rightful place in society, and it was not until she had reached the age of eighteen that she was removed from her convent home and acknowledged by her father. The letter of recognition was duly executed in accordance with the law and registered on the 26th November 1773.

Louison never saw her daughter, or in fact knew of her existence. By the time the young lady emerged from her convent home and was duly acknowledged as the King's child, the Pompadour had passed to her heavenly reward, and her place had been taken by Madame de Barry. The King's new mistress, a woman of considerable acumen and astuteness, suggested a marriage alliance between the Demoiselle Agathe-Louise and her impoverished and needy nephew Vicomte Adolphe du Barry. The King, then ageing and perhaps growing a little senile and completely under the influence of his mistress, at first favoured the proposal which seemed eminently suitable, but the guardians who had been assigned to look after Agathe-Louise objected strongly to the alliance as they considered the Du Barrys to be nonentities who had assumed titles and a birth-right to which neither their birth nor upbringing entitled them; the guardians insisted that 'the fruit of His Majesty's amours had a right to look higher'. This statement seems to have flattered the King and he opposed the marriage, suggesting as kindly as possible that the Vicomte du Barry should look elsewhere for his spouse. In due course Agathe-Louise was married to the Marquis de la Tour du Pin, a member of one of France's oldest and most aristocratic families. Agathe-Louise did not long enjoy married life, and she died in child-bed in 1774; it is extremely doubtful if she ever saw or knew who her mother was.

A Marriage of Convenience

When Louise O'Morphi returned to the King after her second confinement, there were persistent rumours, which had a certain amount of substance, that the power and influence of the Pompadour was on the wane,
and the King no longer had any interest in her. The Pompadour was well
aware of these rumours, and though she tried very hard to dismiss them as
so much Court gossip, she felt uneasy and could not help recalling the
effort of d'Argenson and other enemies to supplant her by the young and
unscrupulous Comtesse de Choiseul-Beaupré, who, she was informed,
having spent some hours in the King's bedroom, burst into the room
where her fellow conspirators were waiting, breathless and dishevelled, and
told them: 'It's all over. I am loved. She will be dismissed. He has given
me his word.' The Pompadour nipped the conspiracy in the bud, and the
Comtesse was banished from the Court and died in child-bed.

Though the Pompadour's power and influence was at a low ebb, there
was no obvious mistress to push her aside, and she did not think that the
King's little Irish demoiselle could ever step into her shoes. A great deal of
the Pompadour's confidence in this regard stemmed from the fact that she
was certain no matter how much the King fussed over Louison, no matter
how much affection he displayed, no matter what gifts he might shower
upon her, she would never be accepted at the Court, which despite its
notable laxity was not a classless society, but an aristocracy which stood
fairly firm on the rock of birthright, even though some adventitious
individuals pierced its armour including Madame herself.

Though the Pompadour was pretty confident and had little to fear so far
as Louison was concerned, she was not altogether pleased when she
considered the amount of time, and the obvious attention which the King
devoted to his young mistress, and the equally obvious pleasure he derived
from his constant visits to her. Never, certainly during the years she had

held first place in the King's regard, had any other woman maintained her hold over the King's passion for so long. Even two pregnancies and the consequent interruption had not impaired or dissipated the King's ardour.

Another thing which worried the Pompadour and caused unease was a growing awareness of her mounting unpopularity among the ordinary people, and the machinations of a fairly powerful clique in the Court circle. Added to her vague fears and feeling of insecurity was the almost calamitous effect of the death of her daughter Alexandrine at the age of ten. Alexandrine was a really lovely girl on whom her mother pinned hopes of establishing a dynasty of her very own. She had no doubts whatsoever that in five or six years time the girl, who had been brought up in a manner befitting a noble-woman, would be married off to one of the aristocrats of France. Such an alliance would not only strengthen the Pompadour's position in the land, but would be the culminating achievement of her life.

The tragic event coupled with the King's interest in Louison brought about a critical state when the Pompadour seemed to balance uneasily on the crumbling edge of a precipice. The doctors who hurried to her aid feared she would collapse and die under the well nigh intolerable strain. Louis XV to his lasting honour was kind and sympathetic. In many regards he was a very selfish and self-indulgent man, but he was kindly and warm-hearted by nature, and there was at times a genuine sympathy in his make-up for those he cared for, or had even a fading regard; perhaps the only one who had forfeited a share in this amiability, partially through her own fault, was his unfortunate wife. In the hour of the Pompadour's distress the King did what he could, in a small way at least, to comfort and sustain the woman he at one time loved, but to a man always needing cossetting, continuous entertainment, satisfaction and some form of escape from his everlasting boredom, the reversed role was something he found not only difficult but almost impossible. It was clearly noted in Court circles, despite his sympathy and apparent understanding, that he sought more and more the company of Louison and spent long hours in her boudoir.

The coming and going of the King to Louison's apartment caused some stir, and rather indiscreetly he made little or no attempt to disguise his actions. The Court was rife with rumours of one sort or another, but most of these were in fact unfounded. Some nobles close to the King and the Court, including many of the more powerful enemies of the Pompadour, felt at this juncture that Louison might be approached and properly briefed to play a more active and decisive part than being simply the King's passive and unambitious bedmate. Indeed if she could be properly

Detail from Venus and Mars surprised by Vulcan (Wallace Collection)

primed and made more useful, the intriguers hoped that the Pompadour might be toppled from her throne and position of power and influence. But the intriguers reckoned without Louison's youth, immaturity, and lack of ability or even desire for high-powered intrigue. Clearly they had no real contact with her or fully realised her shortcomings, particularly her easily satisfied nature and more or less complete lack of ambition or sense of importance.

Some of the more acute and thoughtful observers of the game that was being played behind the scenes, and the whisperings taking place outside the inner circle of the Court, knew very well that Louison lacked the qualities to make her *la grande dame*, and that she would not be acceptable to the majority of the courtiers. They also knew that with all his faults and passions, and God knows they were many, the King's sympathy and feeling for the Pompadour were genuine; that even now when her hold on him appeared tenuous and likely to break at any moment, she held his esteem and affection. This was clearly noted by the observant English ambassador, Lord Albemarle who reported: 'The affliction this unhappy accident has thrown her mother in is almost inexpressible. The trusting attachment His Most Christian Majesty has shown her on this occasion has plainly proved that her favour is not diminished whatever hopes her enemies may have raised upon the French King's fancy for Mlle. O'Morphi.'

As the months passed by and the Pompadour's grief abated somewhat, she returned to her accustomed role of being all things to the King, and at the same time dispensing her favours among a clique supporting her. She built and embellished new palaces, poured out money with a wild prodigality on paintings and objets d'art, and did everything in her power to regain her domination over the King. It was imperative at this stage of reassertion to make sure that Louison was kept rigidly in her place and made to understand that she had one and only one role to play in the King's life, and under no circumstances was she to meet or have discussions on Court or other affairs with those who sought to speak to her. The Pompadour's solution to the problem — with the astute assistance and help of some close friends of the King, particularly his pander-in-chief Lebel — was to revive the idea of Louis's love nest, and from this developed the much discussed Parc aux Cerfs. It has been suggested that the idea did not emanate from the Pompadour or Lebel but from the 'frivolous and corrupt old stallion' the Duc de Richelieu. 'How is it that at sixty-five,' the King once asked him, 'you have the same desires as at twenty-five?' Richelieu who was a notorious expert in the arts of love replied, 'Sir,

I frequently change the object. Novelty produces the desired result.'

In the undermining of Louison's status some subtle tactics were employed. It was carefully pointed out to the King that in time his young mistress might not be so attractive and satisfying to him, that her looks and freshness must inevitably fade, and though she could be used by Louis whenever he desired or wanted her, it would be well to ensure her future by a propitious marriage, particularly if a marriage could be arranged which would not directly affect or interfere with the King's pleasure. Failure to follow this course could give rise to other serious problems for the longer marriage was put off and Louison retained simply for the King's pleasure the more difficult it would be to provide a suitable husband for her. Despite intrigues, subterfuge of one kind or another and a certain amount of malicious gossip calculated to turn the King against Louison, it was soon evident to all that she was capable of maintaining her position unaffected, and though a procession of fresh young grisettes — they had to be young unflowered maidens because of the King's fear of syphilis — were paraded before him and undoubtedly tried, he still returned to Louison who not only satisfied his passion but seemed to arouse fresh desires by her mere presence; further, she could make love as ardently as the King.

Her obvious fecundity did not apparently worry Louis who is credited with siring some twenty bastards, two already by his young Irish mistress and there was to be a third, but it did worry and present a problem to the Pompadour who felt, perhaps with reason, that Louison's love children might bind the King to his young mistress. So far he had shown concern for their welfare and for Louison's well-being, making sure that the pangs of child-bed were minimised and that Louison had every comfort and care in her confinement. This interest and care has not been vouchsafed or chronicled in the case of his other bastards, and such mistresses as the Comtesse de Mailly, Félicité de Vintimille (who bore him a son, Comte du Luc) and Marie-Anne Duchesse de Châteauroux, who enjoined a promise to legitimize any children born of their love-making, were already married before sleeping with the King; furthermore they were aristocrats.

The Pompadour and her friends were growing more restive and anxious and even though the King had returned to Louison in preference to grisettes they persisted in their efforts to prize apart the liaison that had been cemented by many factors including the grudging regard the Pompadour had for Louison and the undoubted delectation of the King. Eventually Louis was persuaded to acknowledge the necessity of providing his young mistress with a suitable husband but not entirely dispensing with her; besides in the very likely event of another pregnancy the question of legitimacy would not be questioned nor even arise. The arrangement pleased all concerned.

Towards the end of the year 1755 and at the age of nineteen Louison was hurriedly but openly married to a dull, unambitious, easy-going but moderately well-off army officer, Saint André Beaufranchet, who was much older than her and could in fact have been her father. Beaufranchet, seigneur d'Ayat, was not quite the penniless man some believe him to have been. He was a professional soldier with few attributes and a land-owner with a sizeable château at Ayat Puy de Dôme. As a result of his marriage to Louison his fortunes changed and he benefited considerably. While the financial reward or dowry bestowed by the King was not small, Beaufranchet's professional career was well advanced, and he was appointed Colonel d'Infanterie Jacquaide, and some little time later for no obvious reason except that Louison may have spoken to the King, he was appointed Major de l'Armeé de Soubise.

Le Prince de Soubise, a fairly honest but mediocre general who com-manded a large French army on the Prussian frontier was a protégé of the Pompadour. He was also a distant relative of Beaufranchet, and was in fact a witness to the marriage, a duty more than possibly assigned to him by the Pompadour, whose willing, almost slavish, tool he was. Besides the higher appointment in the army, Beaufranchet received a gift of bounty of 200,000 livres, jewels or jewellery worth many thousand livres, and a con-siderable sum of money for his wedding expenses.

Louison's marriage lifted her out of her own background, and though Beaufranchet was doubtless aware of the fact that his young and lovely bride had been the King's mistress for some years now it seems he knew nothing whatsoever about her lowly origins. In fact the good soldier was told that his wife was the daughter of a very distinguished soldier whose forebears came from a princely Irish family which fled the country after the defeat and surrender of the Irish army of James II at Limerick in 1691, and he then served with distinction in the army of Louis XIV. Louison for her part forgot the humble cobbler of Rouen and her *maman*, the astute peddler of old clothes in the Place du Palais Royal who had come up in the world and now assumed some semblance of rank as Madame Marguerite Icqui. Louison's own name was actually ennobled in the *acte de mariage* by the addition of the suffix de Boisfailly.

Though now ostensibly a respectable married woman and presumed to be living in her husband's château at Ayat, Louison in fact was not finished with Louis, or more precisely he with her; nor did she live in isolated and lonely splendour while her husband served his King and country in an outpost many days journey from Paris and Versailles. On the contrary as a lady of some rank she was readily available whenever the King desired her, and he had no wish to throw her aside and forget her in favour of the tiresome grisettes provided by Lebel. She was infinitely more satisfying to him and could gratify his need. This happy arrangement continued un-impeded and with the tacit connivance and approval of the Pompadour until 1757. During the last year or so, however, of her friendship and liaison with the King she occupied at least part time, an apartment in the Parc aux Cerfs which a little later became notorious as the abode of the King's harem.

It has been generally accepted and maintained that Louison was installed in the Parc aux Cerfs from the outset of her career as the petite mistress of the King. This, however, was not and is not so. As noted earlier the main proof that she was not an inhabitant or occupant of the Parc aux Cerfs at the height of her liaison stems from the fact that this later notorious esta-blishment in rue St. Mederic was only purchased by the King towards the end of the year 1755; actually the deed of assignment is dated a day before Louison's marriage. A likely though by no means certain connection between Louison and the Parc aux Cerfs is that after her marriage, while still the King's mistress, it may have been her home during the absence of Beaufranchet as Aide-Major to Prince de Soubise on the Prussian frontier.

While there is no doubt Louison continued to be a bedmate of the King after her marriage she may have performed a secondary role superintending the grisettes housed in the Parc aux Cerfs in the guise of servant girls. This was an exercise completely beneath the Pompadour who while approving, nay encouraging, the use of young virgins, would have nothing whatsoever to do with them. The compelling presence of Lebel or any other male procurer was at this time adding to the sea of scandal encompassing the monarchy and the Court, scandals which might be minimised or concealed behind the newly acquired respectability of Louison. While she was not actually a procuress like her mother, she was sufficiently experienced to induct newly acquired maidens and assume the role of maîtresse and groom them to play their expected role of satisfying the King, who still found her his most pleasurable bed-mate.

It has never been satisfactorily explained how the lowly born Louison O'Morphi managed to hold a place in the King's affection and sustain this affection for more than four years, a period longer than that enjoyed by any of his mistresses, noble or otherwise, with the exception of the Pompa-dour and Madame du Barry. The key to her success was possibly to be found in her happy-go-lucky nature and the fact that she was a pretty, alluring creature; she was a voluptuary with a strong passion and capable of loving ardently. Not only could she amuse the King but she could titillate and whet his amatory nature, arousing passions which she could satisfy. Thus there existed a bond between them that was satisfying to both, a fact which did not escape the notice and comments of such worldly observers as d'Argenson, Walpole, Durini and Albemarle.

The End of an Epoch

The year 1756 marked the opening of the Seven Years War, a war in the main engendered by the aggressive designs of Frederick the Great, and the efforts of Maria Theresa to recover the lost province of Silesia from Poland. It was also the beginning of a grand alliance or division of power on the continent of Europe in which France joined with Austria, Russia, Poland and Saxony to curb the ambitions of Frederick and his erstwhile ally, England, now nervously afraid of isolation, and already at war with France in the American colonies.

Though France was ostensibly the main prop of the grand alliance, Louis XV seemed little perturbed by the course of events on the Continent. Life so far as he was concerned ran its normal course; he still devoted a great deal of time and energy to hunting, flitting from one palace to another, and was apparently oblivious of the flood of gross broadsheets and bawdy satires directed against the Pompadour and himself, and openly distributed in the streets and parks of Paris. With war gathering momentum on the frontier, the King's sensuality continued unabated, and was satisfied both by the respectably married Louison and the grisettes now established in the Parc aux Cerfs.

Almost completely removed from reality and deeply immersed in his own narrow preoccupations, the King seemed unaware of the fact that his great military alliance was tottering on the brink of defeat, and was ready to fall apart from sheer incompetence and lack of guidance. The Austrian Ambassador in Paris wrote to Maria Theresa: 'At Court there is nothing but confusion, scandal and injustice. There has been no attempt at good government; everything has been left to chance; the shameful condition of the nation's affairs has caused unspeakable disgust and discouragement, while the intrigues of those who remain on the stage increase the disorder. Sacred duties have been left undone and scandalous conduct has been tolerated.'

In the midst of this confusion, Frederick the Great over-ran Saxony and defeated the Austrians. The English Hanoverian armies under the command of the Duke of Cumberland (who up to this had played a rather passive role and were known as Observers, since they fought no battles but merely observed the turn of events) were growing restive and belligerent. This formerly passive force, faced by a French army under the command of Marshal d'Estrées, heartened by the victories of Frederick, turned to the offensive, but fortunately for France, was heavily defeated and compelled to capitulate by the terms of the Convention of Kloster-Zeven.

The stirring events on the Continent, the long and bloody war sundering Europe and in the end achieving so little, nevertheless played an important part in the life of Louison. The laughing, careless, and pretty mistress of the King, and the wife of a nearly forgotten French officer, for the first time in her life played a strange and what eventually turned out to be a stupid role in the petty but dangerous intrigues which may or may not have had an effect on the course of the war and the fate of Europe. It seems difficult to imagine that the course of history could be affected by a pretty woman who is virtually unknown in its annals, but history has been shaped in this way. What real effect Louison had on events is difficult to determine, but the effect of events on her own life and its future was certainly clear and decisive.

Learning of the petty intrigues and malicious rumours emanating from the Court, the French commander d'Estrées was stirred into action, and a major victory over the enemies of France seemed the only way of establishing his position and rehabilitating himself in the eyes of the King and the people. This sudden urge to action and hope of victory was prompted not by events on the battlefield and the stagnancy of French arms but by events in Court circles.

D'Estrées though a moderately good general, certainly superior to the bloody and gouty Duke of Cumberland, learned that the Pompadour, once more in command of affairs and her Court henchmen were plotting to supersede him. The idea was to hand over the command to the Maréchal Duc de Richelieu, an incompetent soldier and a downright rogue to boot. Though the Pompadour disliked the man intensely he was malleable, and would not stand in the way of promoting her erstwhile favourite the Prince de Soubise to the command of a large part of the army including the Irish brigade, an appointment to which he was not entitled either by reason of rank or ability, and which would be strongly opposed by d'Estrées and other active and more competent commanders. In view, therefore, of the

The Judgement of Paris (Wallace Collection)

plot to depose him, d'Estrées decided that the Court plotters could only be silenced and defeated by a resounding victory for the French army he commanded.

In order to carry out his resolve, d'Estrées advanced quickly through Westphalia, and in the course of the next few days chased the Hanoverian army across the Elbe. His victory however was not sufficiently spectacular to save him from the intriguing clique at Versailles, particularly the Pompadour who had already made arrangements for the promotion of de Soubise; and besides she thoroughly disliked d'Estrées who was an implacable enemy and was unpopular in high places. A continued offensive at this stage by the French army might have ended the war within a year, but many obstacles were put in the Commander's way including a lack of supplies for his troops and the addition of reinforcements. Within a few weeks of d'Estrées pyrrhic victory, Richelieu, because he could amuse the King and was willing to the Pompadour's bidding, was given command over d'Estrées. He had agreed to let de Soubise have thirty-five thousand men — the greater part of his command — and entrusted him with the task of 'liberating Saxony'.

Hurt and angry at the loss of his command which was tantamount to dismissal, d'Estrées hurried back to Versailles to see what could be done by complaint and counter-plot, more particularly the latter, for it was soon clear that the Pompadour was a solid barrier between him and the King. It was now his turn to plot and endeavour by every means at his disposal to supplant or at least discredit the Pompadour. There were many, mainly on the fringe of the Court circle, willing to help him, and the time too seemed propitious, for the people of Paris were in a rebellious mood, not against the King whom they liked, but the Pompadour whom they thoroughly disliked. Venomous libels were circulated and she was apostrophized as 'daughter of a blood-sucker and a leech herself'. Bitter, disgusting and ribald anonymous letters reached her almost daily 'in which obliquity was salted with pornography'.

By some subterfuge Madame d'Estrées managed to ingratiate herself with Louison; obviously she over-rated the more or less minor role Louison now played for she was not as close or as necessary to the King as formerly. More important still she overlooked the fact that Louison's husband had benefited from the change in command and had just been appointed aide to de Soubise in recognition of past and present services to Louis. In this regard it is difficult to understand Madame d'Estrées' interest in Louison unless there was some rumour or understanding that her husband Beaufranchet, who had served under d'Estrées and was a professional soldier, preferred to serve his former commander rather than the favourite de Soubise. Obviously, as already remarked, she must not have been aware of the fact that Louison, though still on warm and friendly terms with the King, did not hold the power she might have exerted a year or two earlier when the position of the Pompadour was at its lowest ebb, and when locked away in her apartment she bemoaned the death of her daughter. Madame had now assumed her former power and authority, and held on to it tightly.

Madame d'Estrées continued her thoughtless intrigue and in due course was on sufficiently friendly terms to be able to introduce her husband to Louison, who received him in her usual warm and friendly way, completely unaware that she was setting up a kind of chain reaction which would change the whole course of her life, and cost the life of her unloved husband. When Maréchal d'Estrées first saw Louison he was struck by her ravishing beauty, her light-hearted smile and manner, and he understood, as a man, the reason for the King's attachment to her. She was a mature young woman, and showed undoubted signs of pregnancy. She received d'Estrées with the natural and simple charm which was so much part of her. She was self-assured, gracefully attired, and gave all the appearance of being a member of French society.

Being an astute man of the world and knowing the ways of the French Court, not to mention the susceptibility of women, d'Estrées played on her natural vanity, pleased her with soft words and extolled her beauty, intimating at the same time that everybody knew the King was still deeply in love with her, and much preferred her to the Pompadour. He managed to convey to her that he had powerful friends at Court, very close to the King, friends who thought more of her and preferred her to the ambitious and dangerous Pompadour, who was endangering the French nation and leading it to defeat. He was able to awaken a germ of patriotism or something akin to it in the young woman to whom France meant very little but Paris a great deal. D'Estrées reminded her that her husband was a soldier of France, a brave man fighting for and defending his country against a host of enemies and these included the Pompadour.

In time he aroused a certain amount of sympathy in Louison, particularly when he painted the Pompadour in the blackest of colours, and insisted that she was the real enemy of France who encompassed the downfall of the country and the Monarchy by placing the destiny and direction of the army in the hands of Le Prince de Soubise, who was nothing more than a venial tool in the hands of an unscrupulous woman who was also plotting against Louison herself.

76

D'Estrées efforts to have de Soubise removed from his command were meeting with support in other quarters, including the Minister for Foreign Affairs, de Bernis, who probably more than anybody else, was aware of the popular feeling, and though closely allied to the Pompadour could not ignore this feeling which was displayed very clearly in the bitter verses and insulting lampoons widely circulated in the streets of Paris, and finding their way into Court circles. Regarding these ugly verses, bitter lampoons and vicious caricatures of the Favourite, d'Estrées saw to it that they were shown to Louison, thus supporting his contention that the Pompadour was an enemy of France and disliked by the people.

Up to this time Louison had neither sought favours from the King nor apparently taken the slighest interest in the Court intrigues, but possibly being a little older and more mature she was highly flattered that a Marshal of France, a man of some importance, and so far as she could see a man very close to the King should show an interest in her and seek her aid. For the first time in her life she felt the urging of a tiny spark of ambition, and began to think that with the help and support of a seemingly powerful section of the Court she could not only undermine the position of the Pompadour but actually take her place.

The future appeared for a moment to be very bright, dazzling almost. Louison promised d'Estrées that she would approach the King on his behalf, but unfortunately she lacked the cunning, the perspicacity, and the mental adroitness to initiate and pursue the sort of intrigue needed to undermine the Pompadour's power. Furthermore, she listened to too many voices and most of the voices lacked any clear-cut plan, and more often than not were at cross-purposes for each *soi-disant* adviser had his own interest at heart. Added to this was the plain fact that she was afraid — certainly scared. After all she had nothing personally against the Pompadour, no real or imaginary grievance, for the Pompadour never obtruded on her life, or did anything, so far as she knew, to turn the King against her; on the contrary the First Lady was a party to the liaison, and had always been friendly, kindly and considerate. Again, there was no valid reason why she should upset or annoy the King who had been good to her, provided adequately for her future, and found her a husband. Equally important, she preferred the comfort and luxury of Paris to the cold and inhospitable château d'Ayat of which her husband was Seigneur.

Despite her impulsive promises to help it was not easy for Louison to effect an opening or present a case in such a way as would arouse the sympathy of the King and make him appreciate the wrong that had been done by the removal of d'Estrées from his command and the chicanery and sophistry which preceded de Soubise's promotion. D'Estrées thereupon instructed Louison to ask the King a question, but had the question couched in such a manner that the simple Louison thought it not only very funny but entirely harmless and innocuous and very likely to amuse the King.

In due course when she judged the moment opportune and found the King particularly friendly and talkative, Louison broached the matter of d'Estrées dismissal. The King smiled and told his young mistress that she should not let matters of state enter into her pretty little head. In the past she would accept the gentle rebuff and forget all about it but, on this occasion she persisted, and when the King continued to laugh and brush her aside in a gentle chiding way, she became annoyed and foolishly insolent, asked: 'What terms are you on now with your precious old girl?'

It was the King's turn to be angry, really angry. He gave Louison one of his freezing looks, and demanded to know what prompted her questions in the first instance, and who had asked her to pry into such matters which were no concern of hers. Breaking into tears, and utterly miserable now, Louison confessed that d'Estrées had confided in her and put the last remark in her mouth. The irate King guessed what was happening and ordered her to leave, and never again come to Paris, or move away from her husband's château at Ayat without Royal permission. The dismissal was noted in Court circles and D'Argenson wrote pithily in his diary: 'The fair one has orders not to show herself in any city.'

Crestfallen and desolate, Louison departed for Ayat; she was so guileless in many respects that she scarcely knew why she had been banished, or how she had incurred the King's wrath. In her exile, for exile it was to her, she hoped against hope that Louis would ask her to return. The weeks went by, however, and there was no word from the King, nor the slightest hint to raise her spirit; the banishment was irrevocable. Louison never felt so miserable, she had no companions but the servants and her aged mother-in-law who would have little sympathy for her. To add to her discomfort she was heavy with child, the King's child maybe, but he would never acknowledge this love child, nor fuss about the accouchement as in the past; after all she was a married woman now and the responsibility rested elsewhere, even if it was the King's child.

Far beyond the quiet and almost unaccessible world of Ayat, the French armies under the command of the Prince de Soubise were marching deep into enemy territory towards the town and citadel of Leipzig. His troops were tired, dispirited, and almost mutinous from the constant marching and trudging through inhospitable countryside during the bitterly cold winter months. All de Soubise's intriguing to obtain a command benefited him little, and the supreme commander, the Duc de Richelieu, more incompetent still, laboured under the suspicion that his subordinate had infinitely more influence at Court and was plotting desperately to supersede him. There was no love lost between the generals, and when in sheer desperation de Soubise asked for fresh reinforcements to bolster up his tired and mutinous army, Richelieu deliberately vacillated, and when at length he dispatched some troops they were ill-trained, ill-equipped, ill-disciplined, and more of a liability than an asset.

Beaufranchet as Aide-Major to the Prince de Soubise shared all the privations of a bitter winter campaign; he must at times have wished he had left the army and retired to the fastness of his château deep in the forests of Auvergne where he could live now in much greater comfort and grandeur than formerly. In the past he was constrained to live very frugally with his mother and a few aged retainers on a small annuity of about eight hundred livres a year. It would be much different now; he could in fact enlarge his estate, and his pretty young wife, whom he had lived with but briefly, would make a most enchanting and delightful châtelaine. All this would be heaven, so much better than the eternal advancing against an illusive army, the slow plodding into the inhospitable Hanoverian countryside with enemies lurking everywhere and deserted homesteads bereft of loot and booty. But all the marching and interminable skirmishing was soon to end when the combined French armies came face to face with the disciplined troops of Frederick.

On the 5th November, 1757, battle was joined at Rosbach. Unfortunately de Soubise, the Court favourite, and in command of a vastly larger army, was no soldier, no tactician even. In the first place he squandered his cavalry in a useless action against the well directed Prussian guns, and in the second place, he failed, ignobly, to stop the Prussian cavalry decimating his infantry, already subjected to a fierce and unrelenting cannonading. When at length the Prussian infantry advanced, the French, already badly shattered, broke and fled. De Soubise penned a heartbreaking dispatch to Louis, 'I write to Your Majesty in a paroxysm of despair. Your army has been totally routed. I cannot say how many of your officers are killed, taken prisoner, or are missing.' This was a cruel blow for the Pompadour who was now subjected to the bitter execrations of the public and the nobility who knew she had supported and advanced the promotion of de Soubise against d'Estrées. What a pity the King had not listened to his discarded little mistress, even though she was only the mouthpiece of intriguers.

Louison was to share in the débâcle of the bloody defeat at Rosbach for among the many officers killed and the thousands left dead on the battlefield was her husband. Seventeen days after the death of Beaufranchet, Louison was safely delivered of a baby boy. In looks the child was not a Beaufranchet but a Bourbon.

Though distances were great, the mountains and forests of Auvergne did not make an impenetrable wall between Versailles and the Château d'Ayat for the King was quickly informed of the birth of the child. The Pompadour, stirred perhaps by maternal instinct or a feeling of pity for the young widow who had served the King well, asked Louis to permit her to adopt the child and have him brought up by her in Court. For some reason or other the King demurred, and though he made provision, Louison was left with her child until about twelve years later when the King ordered that the boy be appointed a Royal Page which could be taken as an acknowledgement of paternity, or at least recognition of noble birth.

Louison apparently settled down and accepted the quiet life at Ayat, devoting her attention to the rearing of her infant son. The Château d'Ayat was in a lonely and remote part of the mountainous and wooded Auvergne. Today it is a village in the department Puy de Dôme, then it was a hamlet locked in the folds of the Col de la Ventouse and dominated by the castellated home of Gilbert Antoine Desaix. Two miles to the north was the hamlet of Randanne with the magnificent château of the Comte de Montlosier, who was a generous benefactor of the Auvergnats, and after Desaix, Louison's nearest neighbour; there was also a small chateau at Theix two miles in the opposite direction. The roads to Randanne and Theix were little more than mountain tracks winding round the lac d'Ayat which had been created by the lava stream which once poured from the Puy de la Vache. It was a lonely isolated country, but Louison was happy enough with her child and the friendship of Montlosier and Desaix.

How far Louison cut herself adrift from her mother and sisters it is not possible to know, but it would seem they had gone completely from her life. There is, however, an un-authenticated sequel to her banishment from Versailles. Rumour would have it that her slightly pock-marked sister Brigitte was installed in the Parc aux Cerfs. Brigitte had little to commend her· but beautiful hands, and must at this time have lost some of the bloom of youth. But the King had reached the stage of insensitivity so far as his pleasures were concerned, and he was no longer particular. But perhaps the plain Brigitte had some of the native wit and charm of her sister to entertain the King — the same wit and charm which enabled Louison to retain the King's affection for so long! Whether Brigitte filled the role of a

Royal grisette or not, there is no evidence to suggest Louison was aware of it, and on the whole it would seem more than likely that the rumour was intended to embellish and round off the story of Louison and her Royal paramour.

A New Beginning

Though banished by Louis, and confined to the loneliness of an isolated country home, Louison was not quite forgotten by her former lover. For most of her life she was a Royal pensioner and received an annuity of about 12,000 francs, thus she remained on a different footing from the ordinary run of girls who amused the King, and were then dismissed with a gift of money, and permitted to live as they wished, marrying whom they chose. This freedom was denied to Louison, and it is doubtful if even in the fastness of the province of Auvergne a lover was permitted to cross the threshold of the Château d'Ayat. Her home was carefully guarded by loyal servants who received their instructions from a Court official. However she was permitted to receive and presumably visit her near neighbours, particularly the family of Desaix, Seigneur de Veyoux, and this is evident from the fact that a few years later her young son was chosen to be the godfather of Louis Charles Desaix who became one of the most distinguished soldiers of France. She was also permitted to visit and receive the Comte de Montlosier and his family.

Though it seemed somewhat harsh that the young widow should be more or less confined to her chateau and guarded from the outside world there was good reason for this. Louison after all had been the King's mistress for four years, and if she chose there was much she could tell about her Royal lover and many in high places, scandal which was eagerly sought by those who disliked the King and even more so the Pompadour. It was necessary therefore to make sure that nobody save those considered safe should have access to her and no word of scandal should escape her lips.

Louison was now a charming and beautiful woman of twenty-two. She was a widow with a sturdy infant son, and was comparatively well off. Thus she was in every respect a most desirable woman, and certainly if she appeared in fashionable Paris circles she would not remain single for long,

Diana et Callisto (charcoal)

nor would she in the ordinary way escape the attentions of some well-to-do lover. Whether the thought of the gay world or marriage entered Louison's mind or not it is hard to say, but it is difficult to imagine this charming, young woman being condemned to the loneliness of a widowed Châtelaine in one of the most remote and isolated parts of the French countryside. Whatever her wishes and ambitions may have been the opportunity for meeting a suitable spouse was very remote. Those close to the King, perhaps the Pompadour, perhaps the King himself conscious of his duty to a former mistress, and now a Royal charge, decided that Louison should not be condemned to widowhood and equally important permitted to marry some man of her own choice. A search for a suitable husband was initiated.

In 1759, just two years after the death of Beaufranchet, Louison was married to François-Nicholas le Norman at the time a Revenue official at Riom, the old mediaeval town which vied with Clermont-Ferrand as the administrative capital of Auvergne and was not far distant from Ayat. Though Revenue officials were rather petty government officers and carried little rank they were known to make quite a considerable income and amass fortunes by devious means. Despite the fact that le Norman was a minor official, he was not quite so unimportant as his position would suggest, for he was in fact a cousin of M. Le-Normand d'Etioles, the Pompadour's forgotten husband, which would indicate that the marriage was not simply one of chance, but had been very carefully arranged in every detail. The fact that Louison could not choose whom she wished or wanted as a husband is vouched for by D'Argenson, who stated that she could not effect any liaison whatsoever without the King's permission, and this is borne out by subsequent events.

When Louison's second marriage was first mooted and all arrangements made for it, apparently with the consent and approval of the King, a hitch arose, and according to the Marquis de Valfons, who was an equerry and very close to the King, the latter on second thoughts withdrew his consent and ordered that the marriage should not take place. Obviously his second thoughts may have been prompted by a desire to bring the pretty widow back to Paris and reinstate her in her former role; a procession of grisettes satisfied his passion, but it required something more than gratification to satisfy his carnality. A messenger was sent post haste to Riom with the King's revocation and an order requiring Louison to remain at the château d'Ayat and not to leave it without permission. For some reason or other, unexplained but pretty obvious, the messenger was delayed and arrived too late to prevent the marriage ceremony taking place in the romanesque church of St. Pierre in Riom.

The Pompadour was pleased and delighted with the success of her plan and the King was constrained to accept the marriage as a *fait accompli*. Louison quitted the isolated fastness of Ayat and settled down with her husband and two year old son in Riom, which if not a lively and pulsating city like her beloved Paris was infinitely better than the backwash and isolation of scattered hamlets in the mountains of Auvergne.

Residence in Riom did not last too long however, and whether the subsequent move to Paris originated with the Pompadour or the King it is difficult to know. At all events some few months after his marriage François le Norman was appointed Trésorier de l'Ordre du Saint Esprit, a high sounding title but none the less an important sinecure carrying with it the position of Treasurer of the Marc d'Or; in simple terms he was the official who levied first fruits on Court and State appointments, a more fitting position for the husband of a former mistress of the King and a cousin of the Pompadour.

The accretion of an honourable title and a worthwhile sinecure meant that Louison could again reside in Paris and assume the role of a lady of quality and, more important still, be acceptable to Society, something which the Pompadour would not countenance in the past despite the King's affection and interest in her. Oddly enough at this particular time, Louison might have played a role in the sex life of the King, but so far as we know she remained outside the confines of the gossiping Court and the debauchery which marked the last decade of her former lover's life. Unlike such scandal-mongers as Madame de Hausset, the Pompadour's personal companion, who thought little of detailing all the scandal, chatter and tittle tattle of the Court, and a host of courtiers like d'Argenson whose intimate diaries exposed the Court in all its unattractive nakedness, Louison maintained a loyal silence. Her silence and loyalty accounts to some extent for the meagre details concerning her life at this period, and but for an occasional reference in an intimate diary and the sumptuous work of the ageing Boucher who still managed to recapture some of the charm and beauty of his former model, Louison behaved with all the nonchalant aplomb of a Parisian lady of fashion.

In April 1764, the Pompadour died at Versailles and that night her emaciated and tormented body was removed to the Hôtel des Réservoirs and lay in a *chapelle ardente* until her funeral two days later. She was only forty, twelve years older than Louison who nearly supplanted her. It was bitterly cold and wet when the funeral cortège of the Pompadour left the Hôtel des Réservoirs for the Convent of the Capuchines where she was laid to rest in the same tomb as her daughter, Alexandrine. A large crowd watched the funeral procession in silence as it proceeded through the Place Louis le Grand to the convent which was razed some forty years later to make way for the Rue Napoléan, now Rue de la Paix. Few tears were shed by the curious onlookers or those who followed the cortège for the Pompadour was far from popular. Though Paris may not have mourned her passing the King was sad, and Louison too may have expressed regret for, on the whole, the Pompadour had been kind to her; perhaps she consciously appreciated the fact that Louison satisfied a need which she was incapable of.

Two years after the death of the Pompadour, Louison was parted from her son to whom she was deeply attached. The boy was ten years old when he was called to the Palace to fill the role of Royal page and companion to the King's grandson, Charles-Philippe who was his own age. Whether this action presaged a plan to instal Louison in the palace or was simply recognition for past services and acknowledgement of the boy's paternity it is difficult to say. Certainly the King had kept in close contact with his former mistress and the installation of her young son in Court supports this fact.

The death of the Pompadour deprived the King of a *maîtresse en titre*, and though his sensuality may have been somewhat satisfied by the unknown grisettes in the Parc aux Cerfs, it was assuming a grossness meriting the rebuke of his confessor. Hitherto, perhaps because of the Pompadour's influence, the Parc aux Cerfs was relatively little known and kept very much in the background. Now, however, it was acquiring a salacious notoriety presenting the picture of a seraglio or private brothel housing a number of maidens for the King's delectation, and the amusement and titillation of his cronies, who chased the naked girls around the gardens in imitation of a hunt.

As if to secure more firmly the bond which existed between the King and Louison, her husband, François, now Seigneur de Flaghac, was appointed Maître d'Hôtel du Comte d'Artois, or steward of the household of the King's orphaned grandson, Charles-Philippe, a robust and unruly boy soon to show signs of the pathological sensuality of his grandfather; he was later to assume the kingship of France as Charles X.

The actual relationship between Louison and the King at this juncture of her life is difficult to determine. Whether she returned to the King in her former role and cuckold her somewhat staid husband neither the diarists or Court gossips record, but it is clearly evident from the favours and honours bestowed that a certain intimacy or warm friendship existed, and the petite

O'Morphil of a decade earlier was still looked upon with favour.

Louis XV has been a lonely soul since the death of the Pompadour and now as a man in his early fifties still required the cosseting, attention and admiration he always had been used to; thus the post of *maîtresse en titre* was wide open to several contenders. It was rumoured too that the King was becoming more and more dissatisfied and weary of his visits to the Parc aux Cerfs and wished for the easy, friendly, intimacy of former days; days made satisfying by the presence of understanding women such as Madame de Nailly, the Marquise de Vintimille, the Pompadour and Louison who was now favoured by the King. For some reason or other she did not attain the role, and whether this was due to a sense of loyalty to her husband or the machination of courtiers it is not known.

Four years after the death of the Pompadour the plebian Jeanne Beçu filled the vacant role of *maîtresse en titre*. Jeanne was very pretty and six years younger than Louison.

With the advent of Jeanne Beçu, respectably ennobled as the Comtesse du Barry, Louis XV had no further need for Louison, though it is more than probable their paths crossed at the Hôtel du Comte D'Artois, where her husband was steward and her son a companion to the young D'Artois when not otherwise engaged as one of the Royal pages. On the other hand there does not appear to have been any contact or friendship between Louison and the Du Barry who combined all the attributes of the Pompadour and Louison so satisfactorily that the Parc aux Cerfs was closed and its inmates discharged. Undoubtedly the two young women knew each other in passing and maintained a tolerable understanding, but it was not until some years later, under more adverse and turbulent conditions, that they came to know each other more intimately, and by then their pasts were submerged in purposeful silence.

Louison at this time was a remarkably beautiful woman, still a worthy subject for the brush and canvas of Boucher who had immortalised her in her youth, and was her first good friend, but the great artist who took her from the back streets of Paris to be his model and bed-mate died in 1770 'among his treasures, seated at an easel before a picture of Venus, the brush fallen out of his hand'. That Venus might have been Louison for we know that when she left his atelier for the bed of a King, he never used a live model again, but relied entirely on his memory to recapture with startling reality the voluptuous young body he knew so intimately and pleasurably in the past.

Four years later on 10th May, 1774, Louis XV died of smallpox, his body so putrefied by disease that no embalmer would touch it, and the Duc de

Villequier, a chamberlain, declared that a lying-in-state was utterly impossible and could not be considered, something most unusual in the history of Kings. Two gravediggers were conscripted to place the rotting body in a coffin which was placed in a larger coffin with the space between packed with lime and camphorated spirits.

The deceased King left few behind to mourn his passing and the former well-beloved was now well hated. Louison, however, felt and experienced a deep sorrow, pain and regret. With all his faults and they were many, the King had squandered a heritage, and was more deeply dedicated to the hunt, the flesh and the smiles and cajolery of his mistresses than the country he had sworn to serve, yet, so far as Louison was concerned she only remembered him as a good man, a nice man. He had always been kind to her, generous too and in his own odd way thoughtful and considerate. She had given her nubile body to him, yielded warmly to his amorous embraces and he had repaid her generously. She would never forget that; nor would she forget the King had acknowledged his paternity of her two children, the little demoiselle Agathe-Louise whom he ennobled and her son Louis Charles who had been placed in the École Militaire a few years before the King's death. This famous school was founded by Louis XV in 1752 as an officer-cadet school for the sons of country gentlemen. We may recall that Agathe-Louise was married to the Marquis de la Tour du Pin; she died in child-bed a few months after the death of her father. A year later Louis Charles graduated from the École Militaire.

A few years after the death of Louis XV, Louison received an odd note which brought back a flood of memories, memories she had hoped were forgotten or at least interred with the bones of her royal lover. In 1783 the ageing and shuffling Casanova returned to Paris where he met Louis Charles Beaufranchet, then a young staff officer at Fountainebleau. He became quite friendly with him and noted in his memoirs that the young man 'did not know the story of his mother whose living image he was'. Though thirty years had passed by since Casanova wrote that 'it would be impossible to see a more consummate beauty than Louison' who then possessed 'everything that nature and the art of the painter could combine in the way of perfect beauty'. He asked Beaufranchet to convey his compliments to his mother, remarking, 'I wrote my name in his note-book.'

The Gathering Storm

The years flowed by swiftly and to some extent calmly for Louison, and though her husband held the stewardship of the Hotel d'Artois he played little or no part in the unedifying life of the young prince, who at the age of twenty-four had accumulated debts of more than twenty million livres and was noted for his inordinate fondness of wine, women and song.

The Paris and Versailles Louison had known in the past was almost a faded memory for under the lack-lustre and impotent rule of Louis XVI the Court was colourless and inept. The King, though popular with the people, lacked all the character of his father and created a division between the Crown and the nobility which paved the way for a future revolution. He was unfortunate, perhaps, in his Queen, Marie Antoinette, who was unpopular with all save a few cronies who clung to her for various reasons. She was a flippant, impetuous and sentimental woman who had nothing in common with her husband and was most unsuited to him in every way. Because of his gross eating habits and his interest in manual work of one sort or another she found him repulsive, and as he was said to be afflicted with phimosis she, naturally, suffered from frustration and turned to pornography, erotica, and mild flirtations as a palliative; little wonder that in later years countless filthy pamphlets accused her of many vices, including lesbianism.

With an indecisive and vacillating monarch, an unpopular, uncaring Queen, a succession of bad harvests and an intolerable national debt there were signs, not perhaps very ominous, of a conflagration, but signs nonetheless marking the creation of the embryo of revolution. Yet in Paris, despite increasing taxation, talks of reform and occasional riots and noisy meetings, the atmosphere was one of proverbial French optimism and natural gaiety.

Louison at this time, though middle-aged, was a beautiful woman; she

Venus and Cupid with doves (*Wallace Collection*)

was wealthy enough to hold her own with the élite of Paris. Her background was forgotten or more likely unknown to most people. As a *grande dame* she carried herself well, and sought to outdo the Comtesse de Valentinois, a grand-daughter of the diarist the Duc de Saint-Simon, who was a leader of fashion, and whose carriage was the envy of Paris, with panels composed of exquisitely painted procelain from the Royal manufactory at Sèvres, the carriage was drawn by dapple grey horses with harness of crimson silk embroidered with silver. Louison, who occasionally boasted of her role as the late King's mistress and of noble Irish ancestry, first assumed by her mother, was not to be outdone by the Comtesse, and had the sides of her coach made of the finest buhl in tortoiseshell and inlaid with brass. The horses drawing her coach were all jet black, and the harness was of crimson velvet and gold. In sheer magnificence and craftsmanship, Louison's carriage parading along the fashionable Bois de Boulogne, rivalled that of the Comtesse who normally set the fashion.

There is perhaps a touch of irony in the rivalry between the two *grandes dames* for according to Casanova it was the Comtesse de Valentinois, a sister-in-law of the Prince of Monaco, who encompassed Louison's downfall, and not Madame d'Estrées. The story is not very different from that already told, save that the Comtesse told Louison 'to make the King laugh by asking how he treated his old wife'. This according to Casanova astonished the King who exclaimed, 'You miserable wretch, who got you to ask me that question?' Louison told the King, and the Comtesse was not seen at Court again until two years later. There is no evidence whatsoever to support this story, and it is in accord with many of Casanova's half-truths.

The daughter of the cobbler of Rouen had come a long way from the narrow alleys of Rouen and the uninviting back streets of Paris. There was no resemblance between the young girl, in her cheap clothes, who was brought by Casanova to Boucher, and the elegant lady driving in her splendid carriage along the Bois de Boulogne. But these displays of wealth and affluence brought their troubles, and it is recorded that the Swedish ambassador apparently by a 'deliberate accident' met Louison in a head-on collision, and drove a shaft right through one of the exquisite tortoiseshell panels of her carriage. The crowd, who were not unduly fond of the former Royal mistress, nor indeed kindly disposed to any of the former Royal mistresses, began to shout and jeer derisively, so 'that Madame le Norman was constrained to drive her damaged carriage home, disconsolate'. Heriz, who wrote these words, is not entirely fair to Louison. Though the crowd very possibly scoffed and jeered at her predicament, it is very doubtful if they knew she was the late King's mistress, or if they were ill-disposed to any of his mistresses. So far as Louison and the others were concerned they were virtually unknown to the ordinary people, and it was only mistresses of the notoriety of the Pompadour and the Du Barry who earned their displeasure. But the people of Paris who saw the well-to-do citizens flaunt their riches and drive in their fine carriages along the Bois de Boulogne were ready at all times to laugh and jeer at any mishap that might befall them, just as a few years later when power fell into their hands, they dragged the wealthy citizens through the streets of the city, subjecting them to every affront and insult. The day of *sans-culottes* was near at hand.

Despite ominous signs, Louison continued to bask in the luxury of affluence and enjoy the life of a lady in high society. Unfortunately for her and the wealthy aristocrats their world was becoming more and more unstable and uncertain. Riots in the city of Paris had become more frequent and there were rumours of bitter clashes between ultra-loyalists and liberal forces throughout the provinces; many provincial towns, particularly Rouen where Louison was born witnessed what amounted to civil war. On the whole, despite the demagogy of near-mad and bloodthirsty men like Marat, Hébert and Robespierre, life in Paris remained relatively serene. One important change had however taken place, the Parlement of Paris had disappeared and an Assembly, in the main dominated by moderates and liberals, ruled the country, for the King, sluggish-minded, diffident, but well-meaning was now only a figurehead — fat, pious and lethargic.

The most ominous sign of impending change took place in October 1789 when an armed rabble marched from Paris to Versailles — a distance of ten miles — demanding food for the hungry people and the head of the Queen who was thoroughly disliked because of her supposed response to their appeal for bread, 'Let them eat cake.' The mob, however, insisted the Royal family should return to Paris. The King agreed and set up his Court in the Tuileries, and at the behest of the Assembly changed his title from being 'by the grace of God King of France and Navarre' to become 'by the grace of God and the constitutional law of the state, King of the French'.

Though much of the glamour, gaiety and insouciance had deserted Paris and an air of uncertainty and suspense prevailed, life for the most part continued in a fairly normal way and this despite the almost continuous haranguing and incitement by rabble-rousing demagogues of the most loathesome type. There were bread riots too, but these were confined to the poorer areas. The near continuous processions of unruly, scrofulous partisans of one revolutionary group or another made firm government more and more difficult. None the less Louison and the *petite bourgeoisie* generally continued to lead the lives they had been used to, and seemed impervious to the portents of the future and what it might hold for them.

As the darkening clouds of revolution gathered, Louison found a certain security in the two men on whom she relied, her son Louis Charles Beaufranchet, now a mature man in his thirties and her husband François-Nicholas le Norman. Louis had made considerable progress in the army from the day he graduated from the École Militaire and was appointed a sub-Lieutenant in the Soubise Legion, an élite corp; a year or two later he attained the rank of Captain of the cavalry regiment of Berri, an equally élite corp. Fortunately or unfortunately most élite regiments had been abolished or abandoned by their officers as the army became an instrument of the revolution, but by 1789 Beaufranchet had reached a high rank in the newly formed National Guard, which now incorporated what remained of the former noble regiments.

François-Nicholas le Norman who was some years older than Louison, was proud of his beautiful wife, but his position as Steward to the house of the Comte d'Artois was far from easy. For one thing the gay young Comte, who was the same age as François's stepson, Louis-Charles, was an inveterate gambler and womanizer. At the age of twenty-four he had accumulated vast debts and was notorious for his sexual activities; a recent writer notes, 'Artois had the pathological sensuality of his house. Not only did he run through all the famous prostitutes in Paris, but he seduced many Court ladies including the Duchesse de Guiche whom the public looked upon as one of his easiest conquests'. As a young man therefore, he almost outshone his grandfather Louis XV in licentiousness, and differed considerably from his colourless brother the King for whom he had the utmost contempt.

Artois had apartments at Versailles but as a young man built the delightful Bagatelle in the Bois de Boulogne near where le Norman had an office and where Louison drove her sumptuous carriage, thus she was well acquainted with the young man who in the heady pre-revolution days was popular with Parisians both rich and poor. Fortunately for le Norman, Louison had reached an age when despite her beauty and amorous proclivity she was relatively safe from the searching hands, the fashionable ease and light amiability of d'Artois which pleased and fascinated so many women.

As the revolution with its plots and counter plots developed, and power swayed uneasily between the diverse brands of revolutionists, liberals,

Girondins, Jacobins and others, efforts were being made by Monarchists to stage a counter coup and restore the Monarch to his former status. The leader of the Royalists in the absence of any initiative from the King was d'Artois, who a few years earlier had fallen madly in love with the beautiful young Vicomtesse de Polastron 'an ash blonde with china-blue eyes, a wonderfully sweet smile and a low voice'. She completely reformed him and turned his mind to more serious matters.

With his master acknowledged as the leader of the Court party and the outstanding Royalist, le Norman was willy-nilly involved, and though his support may have been relatively unimportant the very fact that he was close to d'Artois was bound at some time or other to involve Louison. Her position was difficult and fraught with certain dangers for her son, a professional soldier who was playing his part as a loyal servant of the Assembly, while her husband was loyal to a man who strongly opposed any liberal reforms emanating from the Assembly, and was actually plotting to gather an army of Royalist soldiers to march on the Assembly and arrest its members.

Nothing came of the plot but d'Artois continued to conspire to overthrow the Assembly. Apparently his endeavours had not escaped the notice of some of the more sanguinary revolutionary groups who by speech and pamphlet were arousing the mob and paving the way for a proletarian assumption of power. It so happened that one of these pamphlets found its way into the hands of the King listing 'enemies of the people'. The first name on the list was d'Artois, and feeling for his safety and conscious that his activities might topple the unstaple monarchy, the King ordered his brother to leave France immediately.

That night d'Artois escaped from his apartment at Versailles and fled across the Belgium frontier with a few retainers. Whether Louison or her husband were privy or even aware of d'Artois's plan or whether le Norman's name was on the list of the enemies of the people we do not know, but one thing is certain: le Norman was a sick and troubled man and less than a year later in 1790 he died leaving Louison a widow for the second time in her life; she received a pension of 12,000 francs which with the other pensions and gifts earned over a lifetime left her very comfortably off, though how long this happy state of affairs would last was another matter.

Alone but for her son, Louison was now a middle-aged woman; she had grown a little plump but was still blessed with fine features, sparkling eyes and the roguish smile so effectively depicted by Boucher almost forty years earlier. It was still possible for her to dress in fashion and drive her carriage

Jove in the shape of Diana surprises Callisto (Louise O'Morphi as Callisto)
(Wallace Collection)

95

in the Bois de Boulogne though it was noticeable that less and less sumptuous carriages were to be seen in this fasionable promenade for many of the nobles and bourgeois had fled to the safety of their country estates or like d'Artois had sought sanctuary beyond the frontier, where a host of emigrés waited in the hope of an uprising or civil war which would restore their privileged position.

Despite the unease, Louison could not tear herself from her beloved Paris and so long as her son was near her she saw little concrete reason for uprooting herself. Louis Charles Beaufranchet was at the time helping to organize the newly formed National Guard and had exchanged his old uniform for the red, white and blue uniform and cockade of the army of the Assembly. His promotion as a career soldier was rapid and by 1791 he had risen to the rank of Lieutenant-Colonel, and the following year attained the position of General de Brigade; this rapid promotion was in the main due to the paucity of professional soldiers because of the defection of many thousand nobleofficers. The re-organisation of the army was paramount, for the King at the behest of the Assembly declared war on Austria whose troops were massed on the frontier and whose Emperor, with the King of Prussia, had issued a declaration that the King of France should have all his former power and authority restored to him.

A declaration of war by a torn and divided France would seem on the face of it to be a suicidal move bereft of all reason, but the moderates in the Assembly felt a national crisis might bind the people together and contain the revolution at its present moderate stage. On the other hand the royalists felt that the pitiable French army could never sustain the disciplined Austrians and following a defeat, the *ancien regime* would be restored.

Initially success crowned the superior Austrian and Prussian armies who crossed the frontiers and advanced in the direction of Paris. There were stirring calls to arms and fresh recruits including desperadoes from the communes flocked to the colours. In the flurry and excitement of newly aroused patriotic fervour, Beaufranchet and other loyal professional soldiers worked hard to wield an almost unruly rabble into a disciplined force. Their task was made more difficult by the appointment of political zealots to officer rank and commissioners who suspected the professional commanders of being royalists and placed every obstacle in their way. The situation was not improved by extreme and sadistic demagogues like Marat, Hébert and Brissot whose rabid eloquence incited and intoxicated the mobs from the over-crowded garrets and fetid slums of Faubourg, St. Antoine and St. Marceau, districts known to Louison as a child but now a vague and uncertain memory.

Before departing with his newly formed corps to the war zone Beau-franchet implored Louison to repair to the Château d'Ayat as he could no longer guarantee her safety from the rampaging mobs of *tricoteuses, sans-culottes* and *Marseillais* 'a scum of criminals vomited out of the prisons of Genoa and Sicily'. Louison was torn between conflicting interests; she dis-liked the Château d'Ayat, it was like a prison, tightly and securely guarded by the inhospitable mountains of the Auvergne. She would be alone, utterly alone, and there was something of the Paris *gamin* in her make-up; even in middle age and twice widowed she loved the excitement, the gaiety, the whole pulsating life of the city which was second nature to her.

Even though everything Louison held dear was threatened both from within and without she refused to heed her son's advice. Like many other Parisians she saw no valid reason to flee the city and closed her eyes to what was happening around her. Like many others she felt that if anything should happen it would not happen to her, there was no reason why it should. Despite the fall of the Bastille, the attack on the Tuileries, the massacre of the red-coated Swiss Guards, the constant fury and frenzy of unruly mobs, the men and harridans of the Communes and the impending 'September massacres' the Champs Elysées was 'crowded with strollers of one sort or another. A great number of small booths were erected where refreshments were sold and which resounded with music and singing, pan-tomimes and puppet shows of various kinds were here exhibited and in some parts people were dancing and carousing'. Paris was *en fête*, it was always that way.

Beaufranchet bade his mother good-bye; he might never return. An up-rising during the hot sultry days of August 1792 resulted in the storming of the Tuileries by a mob which was fired on by the Swiss Guard and the nobles guarding the royal family. The courtyard where a few hours before the King and his Queen were walking was piled high with dead and dying *sans-culottes*. The mob was almost defeated and driven from the Tuileries when the King, who disliked blood-shed, ordered the Swiss Guards and nobles to lay down their arms, whereupon they were hacked to pieces by the rabble who decapitated them, impaled their heads on pikestaffs, and flung the bodies into the Seine. Some eight hundred Guards and nobles died and the monarchy toppled in a blood bath.

François Buzot, a young and attractive Girondin member of the Con-vention and a lover of Madame Roland described the mob: 'It would seem as if their leaders had sought in all the slums of Paris and Europe for everything that was most hideous and polluted. With dreadful earthen faces black or copper-coloured, with eyes half sunken in their sockets, they gave vent with fetid breath to the coarsest insults and the shrill screams of hungry animals. Their leaders were worthy of such a following; men whose frightful appearance gave evidence of crime and wretchedness; women whose shameless air exposed the foulest debauchery. When all these, with feet, hands and voices, made their horrible din one would have supposed oneself to be in an assembly of demons.'

The King, Queen and members of the Royal family were confined in a small gallery at the Mènege, the riding school attached to the Tuileries, until their imprisonment in the grim and formidable Tower of the Temple, the fortress and headquarters of the Knights of Malta which was built in the thirteenth century.

Louison locked herself in her house, for the world she had come to know and love was at an end.

Mother and Son

In the midst of the tumult and incredible savagery loosed by the reign of terror, Louison was seized by an armed mob of revolutionists who broke into her house, shouting and screaming obscenities. Fortunately she came to little or no harm beyond a wounding of her pride and possible tearing of her clothes and was simply incarcerated like hundreds of other women in the former churches and convents which had been appropriated or requisitioned to imprison the large number of nobles, bourgeoisie and others who had been arrested as enemies of the newly established Republic. Imprisonment with all its hardships was in some respects preferable to freedom in a city paralyzed by terror, hatred and vengeance engendered by blood-thirsty demagogues, supported and sustained by an intoxicated rabble drunk with power and the looted wine and spirits from cellars of the city.

As the days dragged by more and more prisoners added to the discomfort of over-crowding and made life more intolerable. At the same time some of those seized with Louison were haled before the newly established Revolutionary Tribunal, and in due course made their way to Sanson's over-worked guillotine set up in the Place de la Révolution for the diversion, entertainment and delectation of a mob thirsting for blood.

Following her seizure, Louison was confined in the former convent of Sainte-Pélagie in the Rue du Puits l'Hermite, behind which was the Jardin des Plantes. Ironically enough, Sainte-Pélagie was founded in the year 1665 as a place where wantons, prostitutes and ill-used could find refuge when they were no longer wanted or desired. The convent remained an asylum or prison up to the end of the last century when it was demolished, and with the last uprooted brick there perished an institution briefly hallowed by a strange and motley collection of women who played roles — some important, some not so — in the annals of French history.

Sunrise (*Louise O'Morphi depicted as Nereids*) (*Wallace Collection*)

Most of the prisoners seized on the order of the cold and implacable Louise-Antoine de St. Just, the 'Angel of Death', at or about the same time as Louison, were in the main Girondins, idealistic revolutionists and people of moderation who had been thrust aside by the sanguinary Jacobins who, under Robespierre, Hébert and St. Just, instituted the reign of terror. Among the wives of the Girondins incarcerated in Sainte-Pélagie were Madame Péton, the wife of the Mayor of Paris, Madame Brissot, whose husband was leader of the Girondin party, Lucile Desmoulins, the lovely and brilliant wife of Camille, Madame Holstein, Madame Mont-lesson and perhaps best known of all Madame Roland, a true revolutionist but the *bête noire* of the Jacobin leaders and the power behind a hapless husband who tried to be an honest minister of the revolutionary government, and managed to escape to the provinces where he was a hunted man with a price on his head.

Madame Roland, who had been imprisoned as a *femme suspecte aux termes de la loi'*, a meaningless legal phrase, spent a great deal of her time in her convent cell reading and composing her memoirs which vividly described the last few months of her life as well as an impressive picture of her girlhood at Lyons. From these memoirs we get a picture of Sainte-Pélagie while she was incarcerated there. 'The women's part of the prison,' she wrote, 'is divided into long and very narrow passages on each side of which are tiny cells. Each cell is closed by an enormous lock which a turnkey opens each morning; the prisoners then gather in the corridors, on the staircases, in the little courtyard or in the dank and stinking common-room.' There was over-crowding, a lack of sanitary facilities and privacy which most of the women were used to, and often they were subjected to the vilest abuse from the turnkey and the appointees of Marat's Comité de Surveillance. Most cells contained more than a single occupant, but Madame Roland, being something more than simply a *femme suspecte*, occupied a single cell which was scented with fresh flowers, and she was visited frequently by the gentle Soeur Sainte Agathe, the little nun who prepared her for her first Holy Communion in calmer times.

How Louison fitted in with the strange assortment of women confined in Sainte-Pélagie we can only conjecture. Though her son was a high-ranking officer in the army of the new Republic her background was not unknown to the Comité de Surveillance and particularly that of her late husband le Norman who was closely connected with the Comte d'Artois, the recognised leader of the counter revolutionists. Thus she was numbered among the five thousand or so prisoners rounded up at the outset of the Terror.

Sainte-Pélagie differed in some respect from the other over-crowded

101

prisons insofar as many of its occupants were not Royalists, but in fact Republicans. Further, at the outset it contained but a few men while most other prisons had both men and women. Among Louison's fellow prisoners was the Duchesse de Créquy-Montmorency, Josephine de la Pagerie, or Madame Beauharnais as she really was, who later married Napoleon Bonaparte and became for a while Empress of France; Louis XV's former mistress Madame du Barry, and for a short period a friendly Scottish woman, Grace Dalrymple Elliott, with whom Louison had something in common. Grace was a beautiful woman, some twenty years younger than Louison; she had been a mistress of George IV when he was Prince of Wales, but had spent much of her early life in a French convent. She settled in Paris and became attached to the Duke of Orleans and even remained on very friendly terms when he turned against the Monarchy and actually voted for the execution of his cousin the King, under his assumed common name of Philippe Egalité. She remained a firm Royalist and admired Comte d'Artois thus cementing a prison friendship with Louison.

It was a strange quirk of fortune that threw two former mistresses of Louis XV together, for though Louison knew Madame du Barry it was only in the over-crowded and tense atmosphere of Sainte-Pélagie that a friendly atmosphere developed between them. Whether she was aware that in happier days her first child by the King, the young and lovely Agathe Louise, might have married the needy and impoverished Vicomte Adolphe du Barry had not the young girl's guardians insisted that 'the fruit of His Majesty's amours had a right to look higher' we do not know. However in adversity and uncertain when they would be haled before the Comité du Salut Public, a tolerance and understanding seemed to bind the prisoners together, particularly those with a Royalist affinity.

Madame du Barry had, it would seem, reached a higher social plane than Louison since she was *maîtresse en titre* and was ennobled with the title of Duchess, but her background was just as plebeian as her fellow-prisoner's, more so perhaps, insofar as she was born out of wedlock, being the daughter of a dress-maker and a fun loving monk. However, she was sent to an excellent convent by her mother's employer, a rich contractor who may have felt he could use her when she reached maturity. Before reaching the opulent heights of Versailles Jeanne Beçu was the mistress of a Provencal *roué*, Jean Baptiste du Barry, who farmed out her charms to smart rakes at a profit to himself. A recent writer remarks: 'if she never actually worked in a brothel, she was nonetheless no better than a very high class prostitute, albeit selective and at the top of her profession'. But she was not the only one in Sainte-Pélagie who had slept around, even the pious Scotswoman Grace Elliott had been a mistress of George IV and her friendship with Duc d'Orleans was notorious.

Like Louison, Jeanne du Barry was still pretty in middle-age. She had chestnut hair, expressive dark eyes, perfect features, a graceful figure and a 'splendid bosom'. She was also kind-hearted and good-humoured and possessed the amoral attributes which appealed to Louis XV, who, at the time, informed his crony d'Ayen that he 'was experiencing sensual pleasures of an entirely new kind', in fact she was the only woman in France 'who can make me forget I am nearly sixty'. Had the Pompadour been in power away back then there is no doubt Jeanne Bécu would have been installed in the Parc aux Cerfs. The Pompadour was dead, however, and so too was the King's unloved Queen. Unlike Louison it was possible at the time to impose Jeanne du Barry on the Court, but she was accepted with bad grace; this made her unpopular with the nobles and blessed with few friends.

At the outset Louison and her fellow-prisoners found life tolerable enough in Sainte-Pélagie, even though most of the place had been stripped bare and was lacking in every comfort. Madame Elliott said it was 'a most deplorable, dirty, uncomfortable hole', but she would appear to have been arrested after Louison and did not have one of the small cells with its trundle bed and chair. Indeed within a few days of Louison's incarceration many prisoners were thrown into Sainte-Pélagie, and these comprised a motley lot of ladies of quality and prostitutes, actresses and unfrocked nuns who were compelled to sleep on bundles of straw in the passages. One wing across the courtyard was occupied by a number of male prisoners and this added to the overcrowding in the female section, and placed a tax on the smelly drainage system, rendering life more intolerable. Early in September, with an oppressive heat, a number of actresses from the Theâtre de la Nation were, on the instruction of Robespierre, conveyed to Sainte-Pélagie, and their coming made life more difficult still, for they turned the large recreation hall into bedlam, and as they were unlikely to be haled before the Tribunal they spent their time singing, laughing immoderately and regaling the prisoners and gaolers with ribald entertainment which was offensive to the majority of the prisoners. Fortunately they were released after a short sojourn to make way for people suspected of being enemies of the Republic.

The total lack of comfort, the harshness of the gaolers, and the unsavoury food took its toll in illness. The Governor, in effect the head gaoler, was given a meagre allowance to feed the prisoners. In the main the food consisted of boiled haricots dressed with rancid butter, and raw pickled herrings of which large quantities were given to the prisoners as they were imported cheaply from Holland. This food was supplemented with what was called soup and bouilli, 'but,' as a prisoner wrote, 'we were always sick after eating it. Some of the prisoners thought that it was human flesh which was given to us, but I really think it was horses' or asses' flesh, or dead cow.' Bread when available was rough and made of barley; each prisoner was provided with one wine bottle of water each day for drinking and carrying out ablutions. Prisoners who managed to retain or take some money and-jewellery with them could, by bribing the guards, obtain some of the little luxuries they were accustomed to; if personal servants were free and most of them were, they were permitted to visit their mistresses; this made life a little easier for the better off prisoners and Louison was in this category.

With the removal of the obnoxious actresses and some of the prisoners above suspicion, the lack of comfort was offset to a limited extent by a tolerable community life and the prisoners were permitted to move about within the confinement of the convent walls and enjoy the once well-kept gardens. There was always of course, uppermost, a feeling of insecurity and the uncertainty of when any group of prisoners might be taken away to the over-worked Tribunal and condemned to the bloody guillotine set up in the Place de la Revolution. This sense of foreboding weighed more heavily on some prisoners than on others. Among those who suffered this anguish was Madame du Barry and Grace Elliott wrote: 'She is very unhappy. She used to sit on my bed for hours, telling me anecdotes of Louis XV and the Court She dreaded her fate...'

New prisoners and sadistic guards relayed news of what was happening in the terror-stricken city and the country at large, and while most of the prisoners, including Louison were at liberty when the unfortunate Louis XVI was executed in the Place de la Revolution amid the howls of the mob and the incessant beat of drums, it was only during their imprisonment that the full fury of the Terror was unloosed and they realised the uncertainty of their own future.

The news of the execution of the Queen, Marie Antoinette, in mid-October cast a gloom over the inmates of Sainte-Pélagie. The much abused Queen, they learned, died bravely, even apologising to the executioner for treading on his foot. There was news and rumours too of the execution of husbands and relatives of the prisoners, and then as some of the inmates were taken to the notorious Conciergerie the fears and anxieties of those remaining was intensified. First Madame Roland disappeared never to return to her neat cell where she spent almost the entire day writing, then

Sunset (*The Wallace Collection*)

Lucile Camille whose Girondin husband had been executed a few days earlier; then Madame Petion and the wives of other Girondins were dragged off to the Conciergerie, the 'ante-chamber of death', where men and women who were on trial were lodged for a day or two preceding their execution; this building in which more than three hundred prisoners were hacked to pieces in the early days of the Terror, adjoined the Palais de Justice.

The fears and anxiety of the Royalists was intensified when groups of them were taken away never to return again, among them was Madame du Barry. A few days later the sadistic guards retold in detail the story of her execution to her fellow prisoners. The unfortunate mistress of Louis XV did not face execution with the same bravery and resolution as did hundreds of other women. On her way to the guillotine, jolting over the cobbled stones in the straw covered tumbril, Madame du Barry howled and shrieked, and implored the gaping crowds to save her from the guillotine operated by the coldly efficient Samson.

Louison was shocked when the news of the death of du Barry reached Sainte-Pélagie; after all they both served a King according to their lights, and while the du Barry retired from the scene when Louis XV died, Louison through her husband was associated with the Court and the *Ancien Regime*. Her only hope now lay with her son and if he was still in Paris he might effect her release, but then like the four or five thousand former officers he may have fled the country, or he may have been executed as many of them were.

Louis Charles Antoine Beaufranchet was not dead, however, nor had he fled the country or been demoted and replaced by a revolutionary soldier. Stirred with the same patriotism as such distinguished soldiers as Kellerman, Biron, Dugommier, Joubert and Desaix, he was above all a professional soldier, and when the soil of France was threatened and over-run by Austrian troops and their allies, he held a command as Colonel-in-Chief under General Kellerman. The new army of the Republic, particularly the reformed National Guard had been weakened by an influx of volunteers or conscripts of poor calibre. After suffering a series of defeats, notably at Longwy, Verdun, Mons and Tournai, the tide of battle turned; this was due in the main to the reinstatement of former professional officers for even men like Biron and Kellerman suffered a brief period of incarceration or had been relieved of their duties.

With the turn of the tide, Beaufranchet played a gallant part particularly in the capture of Menin and Courtrai. In the fierce battle of Valmy, which proved a turning point in the war for it brought the Prussian invaders to a standstill and actually forced them to retreat in confusion, he fought with conspicuous bravery which was recognised by the deputies Debrel and Levasseur, who had been appointed by the Committee of Public Safety for much the same purpose as a Commissary in some armies today. Though he had been slightly wounded some months earlier at Famars, Beaufranchet had now fully recovered, and for his part on the field at Valmy he was promoted to the post of Marshal. In the late winter he was posted to Paris as General Chief of Staff of a newly formed army under the command of General Berruyer.

All this happened sometime before Robespierre and the Jacobins had seized power, but now the Monarchy had gone, the King was dead, and the Terror encompassed the entire country. Louison was unaware that her son had returned to Paris following the more or less decisive victory of the French army in the main commanded by pre-revolutionary officers, a factor which induced the Assembly, or more correctly the Convention, to recall some of the professional officers to the capital. Beaufranchet was appointed to General Berruyer's staff, and his presence in Paris while the Terror was at its height was both propitious and fortunate.

The external threat to France had been more or less dispelled by the withdrawal of Austrian and allied troops, but the uprisings in the provinces, particularly in the Vendée, Lyons and Marseilles now posed a serious threat to the Republic and Robespierre's Convention. This threat called for yet another army to deal with the internal situation. The recruitment of a new force fell to Beaufranchet who, on reaching Paris, found his mother's house locked and all doors sealed according to the practice of the local sections of the Comité de Surveillance, so that no enemies of the Republic could be hidden or concealed.

As a professional soldier Beaufranchet went about his task of organizing the gendarmerie of the various departments, then assembled at Versailles, and the raw recruits hurriedly enrolled as national volunteers into a single composite army to fight the rebellion throughout France. It was a difficult task as the national volunteers comprised for the most part an unruly lot, and aware of the fact that he would be ordered to the province at any moment because of the urgency of the situation he used what influence he could to have his mother if not released at least transferred to another prison. He was well aware of the fact that Sainte-Pélagie housed more so-called enemies of the regime than almost any other prison in Paris. His efforts in this regard proved successful and Louison was transferred to the Convent des Bénédictins Anglais, where, he felt, her imprisonment might be more bearable and the threat of death less imminent.

107

While it would seem that Louison was now relatively safe from the clutches of the Comité de Surveillance because of her son's position in the army and the fact that he had just been appointed a member of the Committee of the Ministry of Defence, the increasing violence of the Terror and the elimination of all moderate revolutionists made even his position precarious. Most regular officers were considered suspect and continually watched, they were also demoted and some such as General Biron were imprisoned while their background was investigated; this was done at the instigation of civil deputies who were attached to all army corps. Even the families of serving officers were no longer immune from arrest and many of them were condemned to death. Furthermore, there was always the mob to contend with and it was no respecter of persons.

When Louison was removed from Sainte-Pélgaie, she, on the advice of her son shed her name of le Norman and became simply Louise Murphy thus identifying herself with the other Irish people caught up in the Revolution. Le convent des Bénédictins Anglais was seized by Commissaries in the winter of 1793 and stripped of all its valuables; the tombs too were broken open, even that of James II and his daughter Louisa, in the search for lead and concealed valuables. Despite the bare appearance of the convent, 'it was clean, spacious, and airy with an agreeable prospect and a delicious promenade'. But like all the newly requisitioned places of confinement it was over-crowded, and beds were made up in the workroom, the refectory, cloisters and even the outhouses. The prisoners comprised a motley throng, good and bad, rich and poor; in the main they were Irish, English and Scots with a sprinkling of French, including Madame Dupin, the Marquise de Chastellux, the Comtesse d'Albane and the Duchesse de Montmorency. As at Sainte-Pélagie, the convent was subject to periodical searches, and some of the inmates were dragged away and subsequently executed. But on the whole life was more tolerable than at Sainte-Pélagie, and so long as Louison remained lost in the anonymity of a common Irish name she was relatively safe.

Shortly after Louison's removal to the Convent des Bénédictins Anglais, her son was ordered with his army corps to Tours to suppress the rebellion in Vendée which was threatening to set alight a widespread revolt against the Republic. With the greater part of the French army defending the frontiers, the Vendéans pitted against poor troops were meeting with some success, and were gaining more and more adherents. Beaufranchet served with distinction at the first battle of Fontenay-le-Comte when the Vendéans were defeated. The newly formed Republican army saluted his bravery at the behest of the deputies of the Committee of Public Safety, who referred to him simply as General Dayat, thus stripping him of his bourgeois name. Following this success, he served for a time under General Leigonyer with the coastal army at La Rochelle which it was feared might fall to the Vendéans with the help of naval support from Britain.

Despite a number of victories the rebellion in Vendée was far from stamped out, and Beaufranchet under the command of his old friend General Biron, who had been incarcerated for a short while with his wife in Sainte Pélagie when Louison was there, took part in the second battle of Fontenay. In this battle the Republican troops were defeated despite the resistance of the Infantry of Gironde and the volunteers from Herault and Toulouse, who had been formed into a single corps by Beaufranchet, and were inspired to fight by the haranguing of the representatives of the Committee of Public Safety. Beaufranchet and General Nouvion with a corps of old guards covered the retreat, and thus helped to prevent the victorious Vendéans from following, and perhaps annihilating the defeated army.

For a time it seemed, following a series of victories, that the Vendéans might march on Paris and overthrow the government. Two deputies, young, ruthless, and ambitious were despatched to the scene of the fighting by the Committee of Public Safety, and with the deputies Bourdon and Coupillian de Fontenoy who were equally ruthless proceeded to influse the Republican army with new blood. To do this effectively they degraded the two adjutants and promoted a number of young officers on their own responsibility. Had the changes stopped at this it might have been all right, but worse things were to follow when supreme authority, military and civil, was invested in such leaders as Jean Baptiste Carrier, the ruthless and cruel *noyadiste* of Nantes, whose name was to become synonymous with wholesale sadistic murder. His equally ruthless confreres were of the lower middle classes, coopers, carpenters, butchers, hairdressers, and a motley crew of volunteers, who believed the rebellion in Vendée and elsewhere could only be stamped out effectively by the savage and judicial murder of one in every five hundred of the unfortunate population, whether they were in arms or not.

In this reorientation of the army and as a prelude to a new campaign, it was obvious that many of the former Royalist officers who now swore fealty to the Republic and had fought bravely in its defence would be demoted, purged and perhaps imprisoned as they would have been opposed to the wholesale brutality and slaughter suggested, nay ordered, by the Deputies attached to their corps in order to bring the Vendéan rebellion to a speedy end. Beaufranchet's commander was replaced by Antoine Santerre, the rabble rousing Paris brewer and the idol of the mob of Faubourg St. Antoine, whose battalion of Enfants Trouvés carried out the assault on the Tuileries which encompassed the downfall of the Monarchy. Santerre had been elected Commander-in-Chief of the National Guard and got along with the old officers so long as they carried out his orders.

The deputies of the Committee of Public Safety were somewhat different and infinitely more ruthless, for they doubted the loyalty of any of the old guard and insisted on their removal. Biron, one of the ablest French generals, was deprived of his command, and a goldsmith named Rossignol, a trusted revolutionist, took over. He appointed his own staff officers, who included a printer named Momori, and the low comedian Grammont. As General Biron had been removed from his command, his staff officers, including Beaufranchet, were relieved of their duties. Beaufranchet was fortunate in that he suffered no more than deprivation of his rank, but if the ruthless Jean-Baptiste Carrier, a wild madman whose massacres in the provinces exceeded the Terror in Paris, and who on one occasion stripped naked some hundreds of men and women and then bound them together as copulating couples and threw them in the river, had his way Beaufranchet would have been killed with his fellow staff officers. In December 1793, Carrier wrote to the Committee of Public Safety from Nantes, 'I emphatically recommend to the national vengeance those counter revolutionary scoundrels Beyser, Baco, Beaufranchet and Letourneaux; the heads of these four criminals can never heal the deep wounds they have dealt this country ... Condemn them to death and appoint the execution in Nantes.'

Beaufranchet as a private citizen hurried back to Paris with the hope of obtaining his mother's release and then seeking the comparative safety of the Château d'Ayat. When he reached the city he found that he was powerless in the face of the terror prevailing and went into hiding.

A Marriage Interlude

The winter of 1793 was bitterly cold and the inmates of the Convent des Bénédictins Anglais suffered because of lack of fuel. The garden was stripped of its trees, and as most of the prisoners had either been hurriedly seized or, like Louison, transferred from other prisons they had little in the way of warm clothing. Perhaps the greatest hardship suffered by the prison inmates was the over-crowding. At one period there was scarcely room to move about in comfort and each day the beds in the public rooms had to be moved to one side to permit the use of the refectory and main hall. As the months went by, however, the number of prisoners decreased; most had been released when their loyalty was proven, but a great number were victims of the guillotine.

The Christmas of 1793 was celebrated by Louison and her fellow-prisoners, but it had no religious significance, for about the beginning of December the chapel was desecrated by the Commissionaires who removed all the sacred vessels, and the chaplain, the Rev. Father Nailor was taken away. The nuns of the convent, however, managed to maintain some semblance of a community, and though they exerted no authority, nor were they in any way responsible for the prisoners, since they too were prisoners, they proved a source of comfort to the inmates. Shortly after Christmas the nuns were constrained to discard their religious habits, and were no longer permitted to carry out their religious exercises as a community.

Early in the new year a number of prisoners had been removed and this resulted in a little more comfort for those remaining. A new concierge had also been appointed, and despite the visits and inspections by Commissionnaires who carried out ruthless searches, life became more tolerable. Though the worst horrors of the reign of Terror had passed, there was still no certainty among the prisoners that they might not be dragged before

111

the Tribunal and suffer the same fate as the King and so many of his subjects.

It is not known when, exactly, Louison was released from captivity and the records certainly indicate that she was still an inmate of the convent in February 1794. In July of that year all the nuns were removed during the night in six coaches and incarcerated in the Castle of Vincennes. Following the fall and execution of Robespierre the reign of Terror more or less came to an end with a mild reaction against the terrible excesses of the past eighteen months; even on the floor of the Convention many deputies supported the demand 'Justice pour tout le Monde' and called for an end to the executions. By mid-December most of the prisoners had been released, except those who had been sentenced to varying terms of imprisonment by the tribunals. Louison must have been among those released at this time for she certainly never appeared before any tribunal, nor had she been charged with any offence.

On her release, after almost two years imprisonment, Louison returned to live quietly and pick up the threads of her former life in her old home in Paris, but quite clearly life was not going to be the same as formerly. Nevertheless she had much to be thankful for, even though the glamour and ostentatiousness of the past had disappeared and she no longer enjoyed the very adequate pension bestowed upon her by a grateful King whom she satisfied and made happy. Though deprived of her pension she was by no means a poor woman, for like many other wealthy people she managed to retain jewels and chattels and they were more precious than the debased and fluctuating currency.

Life was not cheerful or even certain throughout the winter of 1794. The streets were almost empty of carriages, for few cared to flaunt their rank by driving in public. Dress was simple, often slovenly and most people to show their sympathy with the revolution continued to wear the black wigs, the red caps, the sailors' jackets and the pantaloons of the *sans culottes*. Food was scarce and dear and the women fought for it in the shops and market places. To live in a nice house and experience freedom really meant little for the future was just as uncertain as incarceration in Sainte-Pélagie or the Convent des Bénédictins Anglais. *Egalité ou la mort* was daubed on many walls and on house fronts as 'a constant reminder of the seriousness, if not the precariousness of living'.

Louison did not remain long in Paris for Beaufranchet insisted that not only would she be safer but food and relative comfort could at least be guaranteed at the Château d'Ayat to which she repaired. The Revolution so far as Auvergne was concerned and particularly in the mountain villages almost passed unnoticed. The peasants were devoutly religious, and though in many places they had revolted against the local seigneur, seized part of his lands, stripped his barns, looted his cellars and larders and often indeed destroyed the château, few agitators were to be found in the area, thanks mainly to the generous and enlightened spirit of the Comte de Montlosier who had always been a friend and benefactor to the Auvergnats. Besides, there was little land to divide in this mountainous area, and the patriarchal system seemed to endure despite numerous laws abolishing the *droits seigneuriaux*.

The fall of Robespierre and the eventual abolition of the *Convention* by a new constitution, which set up the *Directoire*, changed the whole aspect of the Revolution. Towards the end of the year 1798, shortly before the coup of Napoleon, Beaufranchet's former military service was recognised, and he was appointed a member of the newly formed Administrative Council of Military Hospitals; this was followed by his appointment as Director of the Military Hospital at Méyières.

Following her son's new appointment, Louison returned to Paris and settled down in her old home. Left to her own resources and though now a woman of sixty she once more embarked on matrimony. Normally one might think that at this time of life, particularly after a strangely adventurous career, she would have been content with her lot, but there must have been something in her character and personality, even at this age, that attracted men to her. We gather that though she was somewhat plump, she was still attractive and looked considerably younger than her years; she also retained some of the oddly innocent coquetry depicted by Boucher more than forty years earlier, and the beauty and loveliness which captivated Louis XV. We can take it too, despite the passing years and a certain amount of hardship, she still retained the charm and naturalness that was her birthright.

Louison's new husband was one Louis Philippe Dumont, député du Calvados, a young, enthusiastic revolutionist and firebrand, who was more than twenty years her junior. Dumont had been deputy delegate of his department to the Convention and to the famous Council of Five Hundred. He was, it would seem, an astute man, and when the tide turned against Robespierre be became a bitter anti-Jacobin, and wrote a scathing pamphlet against them. He was also a bitter and avowed revolutionist and had issued a pamphlet on the punishment to be imposed on the unfortunate Louis XVI which would put him on the side of the Jacobins rather than with the more moderate Girondins.

Dumont earned a slight notoriety as a fervid anti-clericalist, and some of his views in this respect were printed in a pamphlet entitled *A proposal to unite the Parish of Neuville to that of Andouille*. Because of his strong anti-clerical views and undoubted bitterness, Louis Philippe Dumont had been mistakenly identified with a namesake, André Dumont, who was also a deputy to the Convention and a member of the Committee of General Security; he too voted for the King's execution, persecuted the Girondins, and later demanded the death of his former leader Robespierre. Like Louis Philippe, André was a bitter anti-cleric, and when posted to the Department of the Somme caused some two hundred people, sixty-four of whom were priests, to be thrown into the river.

It is extremely hard, puzzling really, to understand what prompted or what reason lay behind this strange and seemingly incongruous marriage. Even though Louison was still beautiful she was past the age when her sexual urges and the need for gratification would be an impelling cause for marriage, nor can one imagine for a moment that love, in any shape or form, played a part in this strange alliance. That she was a lonely woman unused to living alone and in need of protection seems also unlikely since it is probable that at this stage of her life her son was close at hand if not at times living in her house; he was also deeply attached to his mother and would see that she was provided with servants and most of the comfort she formerly enjoyed.

While there may have been some valid, but not clear, reason for Louison to marry it is more difficult to understand why Dumont embarked on the course he did. After all he was a relatively young man and there were many pretty women in Paris whom he could marry. So far as we know he was not a penniless adventurer spewed up by the revolution, nor was he lacking in ability to carve a niche for himself in the hierarchy of the new French aristocracy born of the revolution. One reason that comes to mind was an urgent need for Dumont to bury his not too savoury revolutionary past behind a bourgeois facade, especially now that the Republic had swept its bloodiest and most brutal past under the carpet, and with the establishment of the *Directoire* had become respectable.

Whatever the reasons for the marriage, and they may have been perfectly valid, as for instance a young man's love for an older woman, or the rekindling of a warm passionate nature on the part of a woman who had always been attracted to men. Louison needed men and could over the course of a lifetime recall a succession of them: there was Boucher, Louis XV, Beaufranchet, Francois le Norman and now Philippe Dumont. Her lovers were by no means nonentities, nor the acquisitions of a *demi-monde*; indeed she was particular, and in the days of poverty refused the

114

advances of Casanova, though she did permit him to caress her then lissome body.

From the outset it was evident that Louison's marriage was not likely to endure, so a few years later in the spring of 1800, Dumont petitioned for a divorce and readily obtained it.

Unbroken in heart, Louison accepted as a matter of fact what was at most a blow to her pride and retired gracefully to her own home. Though now without a husband, she was not one to bemoan her past and settled down to live the life of an ageing recluse. On the contrary blessed with vibrant health and vitality as well as an insatiable interest in the world about her, she accepted life as she found it and fortunately for her a semblance of the life she had known in the past was evolving under the aegis of Napoleon Bonaparte's *Directoire*.

In 1803, Louison's son retired from the army with the rank of General. In the same year the Senate elected him Deputy Commissioner to the legislative corps of the Department of Puy-de-Dôme, the Department which embraced the Château d'Ayat. Always a soldier at heart, Beaufranchet took little interest in the Assembly which like most parliamentary institutions of the period was a mere facade, a rubber stamp giving a sense of legality to the dictates of the First Consul. But so far as Louison was concerned there was a certain *éclat* in the honour conferred upon her son and she was quite happy to bask in the aura.

With the Republic now firmly established, a new star dominated the French scene in the person of the former Corsican soldier Napoleon Bonaparte who had taken over the reins of government as First Consul. While he fought the enemies of France with one hand he effected a completely new revolution at home.

In this revolution which was bloodless he returned to something close to the monarchy of the *Ancien Régime*, and appeared to abrogate the principle of the sovereignty of the people proclaimed at the outset of the revolution in the *Déclaration des Droits de l'Homme*. He even created a new nobility and tried to revive the Court. Nowhere were the new changes more apparent than in the Paris which Louison had known from her childhood days, the gay, sparkling city, which she loved, even in her old age, more than the château which she had now abandoned in Auvergne. This city, so much part of her life, was being transformed, being rebuilt and refurbished so that it became more beautiful each day. The new elegance and grace, the salons and soirées were reminiscent of a past which to her was memorable, and once again she could drive in her carriage through the Bois de Boulogne and excite the curiosity of the passers-by.

Envoi

The years slipped by quickly into a new century and a new era, and with the passing years Louison grew old gracefully, living for the most part with her memories and with a past which she sedulously guarded as a precious secret, a secret which she would not share with Louis Philippe Dumont. Indeed few if any knew of her past and the gracious, old lady lived quietly and was known simply as Madame Marie Louise de Beaufranchet le Norman.

Life was now comparatively quiet and peaceful so far as Louison was concerned though all Europe was ablaze with the wars carried to its farthest corners by the all conquering Bonaparte. If the Napoleonic wars made any impact upon her it was only to remind her of other wars and other people, of de Soubise, d'Estrées, Richelieu, the Pompadour, the bloody battle of Rosbach, and the great mistake she had made in 'bothering her pretty, little head with matters that should not concern her'. That was all past now; just one of the bad memories best forgotten.

In spite of war, Paris was a gay city again, enlivened with numerous noisy celebrations of victories, and though the drain on the nation's coffer was great, a new and really beautiful city was arising on all sides. Yet for the old lady driving in her carriage and watching the crowds go by life must have been a little lonely for with the passing years her world had completely disappeared. So too had almost all the friends of her former days. Even her lovely sisters who had been brightly burning stars in the glamorous demi-monde of half a century earlier were now completely forgotten. Louison might remember them — the gay, light-hearted and really beautiful Marguerite, the plain, pock-marked Brigitte, the lovely and attractive Madeleine who might but for the uncertain vagaries of the theatre have made a name for herself at the Opéra-Comique, and Victoire who loved Boucher before she did, filled his most lascivious canvas

'L'Odalisque', and figured in the witty and scandalous memoirs of Casanova as she did herself. They had all vanished from her life, disappeared many years ago and were but dim reminders of her own lowly background.

There were numerous nephews and nieces, but Louison never knew them. Had she known them they might have been a solace in her lonely old age, but fate decreed that her path through life was not theirs, and their footsteps would never cross.

Whilst General Beaufranchet lived his mother had somebody to turn to, somebody whom she could lean upon for there is no doubt that a deep and abiding love existed between mother and son, and that but for him she might have suffered the same fate as Madame du Barry.

Beaufranchet died in 1812, the year of the great retreat and the humiliation of Napoleon Bonaparte. He was no longer an active soldier, but had for some years prior to his death held the post of Inspector-General of the horse breeding studs of France. Then, as today, France was renowned as a horse breeding country, and almost a century earlier the King had established a national stud for the purpose of breeding not only good racing horses, but hunters and officers' mounts from pure Arab stock. Even during the worst days of the Revolution when nothing was inviolable, the stud was maintained intact. Beaufranchet was fifty-one when he died; he had never married, but was devoted to his mother and to his God-child Louis Charles Desaix who bore his names and was a distinguished French General.

On the 6th April, 1814, the Emperor Napoleon who had crowned himself in Paris some ten years earlier abdicated at Fontainebleau following his disastrous Russian campaign and defeat at Leipzig. He was exiled to Elba and the Bourbon dynasty was restored in the person of Louis XVIII, a brother of the ill-fated Louis XVI and an uncle of the Dauphin, the 'prisoner of the Temple'.

These were exciting days, days of processions and celebrations for the way was being prepared for the new King by the triumphal entry into Paris of his popular brother, the Duke d'Artois. Nearly thirty years had passed since Louison knew him when her husband Francois-Nicolas le Norman was steward to the Duke's household. He was a gay, light-hearted young man, then, something of a libertine. Now as he rode into Paris, a Prince, preparing the way for his brother, he was kingly in appearance and a superb horseman; the people loved him, and went mad with joy.

A few weeks later the King entered the city; his entry was rather an anticlimax for the Duke d'Artois had been more impressive and had ridden at the head of a vast concourse while 'the King sat heavily in a carriage drawn by eight white horses, his portly figure clothed in an odd mixture of garments of the pre-Revolutionary style and of English fashion'. The crowning ceremony in Notre Dame was followed by a triumphant procession through the city.

Though the restoration of the Bourbons to the throne of France was far from the minds of most Parisians, the streets were crammed with a joyous and enthusiastic crowd who cheered the inordinately corpulent, apopleptic and gout-ridden King who was almost a foreigner to them. Even Chateaubriand was wont to say, 'When I describe the royal family to my countrymen it was as though I had enumerated the children of the Emperor of China.' Much of the cheering and joyous celebration however was the outpouring of a people sick and tired of war, and glad of a peace unknown to them since the start of the revolution twenty-five years earlier; to many it had been almost a lifetime of strife.

Propped on a couch by a window overlooking the processional route was an old woman. She was Marie-Louise de Beaufranchet le Norman, sometimes Marie-Louise Morphy de Boisfailly, but to a King of France and to a great painter she was simply Louison. She was seventy-seven years old now, alone with her fading memories. Vaguely she could recall such processions as this but they happened more than sixty years ago when her lover Louis XV, a grandfather of the King, drove through the crowded streets of Paris in his seemingly endless move from palace to palace; indeed she may have thought vaguely had the course of events in the past been a little different she might have driven in such a procession. That was all past history and she had lived through it — the long reign of Louis XV, the nineteen years in which his grandson sat upon a shaking throne; she had lived through the years of Revolution, through the *Directoire*, through the reign of the Emperor Bonaparte, the years of war, and now a new King — and peace.

Long before the cheering and shouting throng was born, she shared a King's favours with one of the great courtesans of history and she had been very lovely. But now the flame was flickering feebly, very feebly, and with the dawn of a new year Louison died on the 17th January, 1815.

If there was a tombstone raised in the cemetery of Père Lachaise to Louison's memory, it has perished with the years, but the memory of her beauty has been preserved for all time in Boucher's immortal 'Louise O'Morphi sur an Divan' and the other great pictures he painted. What more perfect memorial could she have?

Works Consulted

Alger, John G.: *Englishmen in the French Revolution*. London 1889.
Argenson, Marc-Pierre, Comte d'.: *Mémoires*. Paris.
Bidou, Henry.: *Paris*, London 1939.
Cailleux Jean: *François Boucher, 1703-1770*. Paris, 1964.
Cailleux Jean: 'Who was Boucher's Best Beloved?' *Burlington Magazine*. February 1966.
De Heriz, P.: *La Belle O'Morphi*. London. 1947.
Dictionnaire de Biographie Française: Paris. 1951.
Fenaille, J.: *François Boucher*. Paris. 1880.
Fleury, Comte de.: *Louis XV Intime et ses Petites Maîtresses*. Paris, 1899.
Gaxotte, Pierre: *The French Revolution*. London. 1932.
Gooch, G.P.: *Louis XV* London. 1956.
Hare, Augustus: *Paris*. 2 Volumes. London. 1900.
Hausset, Madame du: *Mémoires*. Paris. 1824.
Hayes, Richard: *Irishmen in France*. Dublin. 1932.
Kahn, Eustace: *Boucher*. Paris. n.d.
Kunstler, Charles: 'La vie quotidienne sous Louis XV.' Paris. *La Révue Bleue*. 13th September 1890.
Lefebire, George: *The French Revolution from its origins to 1793*. London. 1962.
Leys, M.D.: *Between Two Empires*. London. 1955.
Lough, John: *An Introduction to 18th Century France*. London. 1960.
MacFall, Haldane: *Boucher, 1703-1770*. London. 1908.
Mantz, Paul: *Boucher, Lemoyne et Natoire*. Paris. 1880.
Mathiez, Albert: *The French Revolution*. London. 1927.
Mitford, N.: *Madame de Pompadour*. London. 1954.
Nolhac, Pierre de: *François Boucher*. Paris. 1925.
Nolhac, Pierre de: *Louis XV et Madame de Pompadour*. Paris. 1904.

Palmer, A.W.: *A Dictionary of Modern History, 1789-1945*. London. 1962.

Perkins, J.B.: *France under Louis XV*. 2 Volumes. London. 1897.

Pernoud, G., and Flaisser, S.: *The French Revolution*. London. 1960.

Stephens, H.M.: *A History of the French Revolution*. 2 Volumes. London. 1891.

Thompson, J.M.: *The French Revolution*. Oxford. 1947.

Trouncer, Margaret: *The Pompadour*. London. 1956.

Louison

The Life and Loves of Marie Louise O'Morphi

LE DÉSIR DE PLAIRE.

Louison